The Renewed Homiletic

The Renewed Homiletic

O. Wesley Allen Jr., Editor

David Buttrick | Fred B. Craddock

Eugene L. Lowry | Henry H. Mitchell | Charles L. Rice

Fortress Press

Minneapolis

THE RENEWED HOMILETIC

Library of Congress Cataloging-in-Publication Data
The renewed homiletic / O. Wesley Allen, Jr., editor.
    p. cm.
Proceedings of a conference held in fall 2007 at Lexington Theological Seminary.
Includes bibliographical references and index.
ISBN 978-0-8006-9656-6 (alk. paper)
1. Preaching—Congresses. I. Allen, O. Wesley, 1965-
BV4202.R46 2010
251—dc22
                            2009046738

14 13 12 11 10   2 3 4 5 6 7 8 9 10

Contents

Contributors

The New Homiletic

David Buttrick is the Drucilla Moore Buffington Professor of Homiletics and Liturgics, Emeritus, at Vanderbilt University Divinity School. Building on years of earlier essays and research into the way in which people listen to sermons, Buttrick's book, *Homiletic: Moves and Structures* (1987), offered a phenomenological approach to preaching directed toward creating a communal consciousness by a sermonic structure composed of moves.

Fred B. Craddock, an ordained minister in the Christian Church (Disciples of Christ), is the Bandy Distinguished Professor of Preaching and New Testament, Emeritus, in the Candler School of Theology, Emory University. In 1971, with the publication of his first of many works in homiletics—*As One without Authority*—Craddock initiated a paradigm shift in homiletics by presenting an inductive approach to preaching. Craddock played out the implications of this approach in *Overhearing the Gospel* (1978).

Eugene L. Lowry, an ordained United Methodist minister, is the William K. McElvaney Professor of Preaching, Emeritus, at Saint Paul School of Theology. In *The Homiletical Plot* (originally published in 1980) Lowry took vague talk about narrative preaching and gave it a concrete structural expression in what has come to be known as the Lowry Loop. His understanding of narrative preaching has evolved through many books and essays, perhaps most important of which is *The Sermon: Dancing the Edge of Mystery* (1997).

Henry H. Mitchell, an ordained Baptist minister, was Professor of Homiletics and History and Dean of the School of Theology at Virginia Union University. His first homiletical work, *Black Preaching* (1970) explored the history and character of black preaching. This descriptive piece funded a prescriptive work, *The Recovery of Preaching* (1977). In *Celebration and Experience in Preaching* (1990), which brought together and expanded upon themes from these earlier works, Mitchell offered an approach of preaching to the whole person (not just our rational side but also our emotional side), in which sermons move congregations to a climactic celebratory experience of gospel.

Charles L. Rice, an ordained Episcopal priest, is Professor of Homiletics, Emeritus, at Drew Theological School, Drew University, where he taught for thirty-two years. In various early essays—*Interpretation and Imagination* (1970) and *Preaching the Story* (1980), which he coauthored with Edmund A. Steimle and Morris J. Niedenthal—Rice offered an approach in which the use of art, especially telling the stories of human experience, allows hearers to experience the biblical text. His concern for a holistic approach to human experience has extended his focus to the relation of proclamation and liturgy, as evident in his work *The Embodied Word: Preaching as Art and Liturgy* (1991).

The Next Generation

O. Wesley Allen Jr., Professor of Homiletics and Worship, Lexington Theological Seminary

Ronald J. Allen, Nettie Sweeney and Hugh Th. Miller Professor of Preaching and New Testament, Christian Theological Seminary

Dale P. Andrews, Martin Luther King Jr. Professor of Homiletics and Pastoral Theology, Boston University School of Theology

Valerie Bridgeman, Associate Professor, Hebrew Bible/Homiletics and Worship, Scholar in Religion and the Arts, Lancaster Theological Seminary

Gennifer Benjamin Brooks, Ernest and Bernice Styberg Associate Professor of Homiletics, Garrett-Evangelical Theological Seminary

Cláudio Carvalhaes, Assistant Professor of Worship and Preaching, Louisville Presbyterian Theological Seminary

Richard L. Eslinger, Vice President for Academic Affairs/Dean, Professor of Homiletics and Worship, United Theological Seminary

Ruthanna B. Hooke, Assistant Professor of Homiletics, Virginia Theological Seminary

Pablo A. Jiménez, Consultant Editor, Chalice Press

Eunjoo Mary Kim, Associate Professor of Homiletics, Iliff School of Theology

Alyce M. McKenzie, Associate Professor of Homiletics, Perkins School of Theology, Southern Methodist University

Mary Alice Mulligan, Affiliate Professor of Preaching and Ethics, Christian Theological Seminary

Acknowledgments

When I was a sophomore in college in January, 1985, I asked my professor, Earl Gossett, to lead me through an independent study of preaching since I hoped to be appointed as a student pastor in the summer of that year. His first response was negative because, he said, no one without an M.Div. should lead a congregation. I should have listened to him, but I did not and pestered him about the course until he finally said, "Hell, let's do it. Let's keep you from doing any more damage than you're going to do." And then the first piece of damage control he had me read was Fred Craddock's *As One without Authority*. I had grown up listening to only a handful of preachers throughout my youth and had only preached three times at that point (if you could call what I had done preaching). I had not reflected on a homiletical theology or methodology at all. To be honest, at the age of nineteen, I understood little of what I was reading. And yet with that book, I fell in love with preaching and the study of preaching.

While I was working on my Master of Divinity, Bill Muehl and Harry Adams introduced me to the work of Henry Mitchell and Eugene Lowry. When I was working on my Ph.D. at Emory, Fred Craddock told me I could not be a serious homiletician without reading David Buttrick. As a young scholar and college chaplain, I worked to expand my knowledge of the breadth of the homiletical canon and met Charles Rice, and then had the wonderful privilege of following in his footsteps at Drew for too brief a time. With each of these, my love for preaching and the study of preaching deepened.

I have grown to hold conversation as one of my highest theological, pedagogical, and methodological commitments. My internal conversation about the task of preaching has been a fruitful one because so much of it has been with these scholar-preachers. It is difficult to name how indebted I am to them for forming me as a preacher, teacher, and scholar. To say that among preachers and homileticians is cliché, however. All of us who today stand in the pulpit or in the lectern preparing students to enter the pulpit have derived much of what we offer from conversation with the New Homiletic.

The opportunity arose to realize this internal conversation with a face-to-face gathering of Rice, Mitchell, Craddock, Lowry, and Buttrick at Lexington Theological Seminary in the fall of 2007. As Dr. Lowry named in his lecture, these men had all followed each other around preaching and lecturing in the same schools, conferences, and churches, but they had never all shared the podium together. And the seminary brought them together to reflect on the implications of their early work, classified as the New Homiletic, for the twenty-first century. We called the conference *The Re(New)ed Homiletic*. It was more than just an honor for me to be a part of this. Henry's wife, the late Ella Mitchell, herself an esteemed scholar-preacher whom I wish had lived to see this book completed (may God continue to bless her as she has blessed us), stared into my face during a meal at the conference and said to me, "You look like your dreams have come true." She was right.

And there are many people to thank for making this dream come true. The faculty, administration, staff, and students at Lexington Theological Seminary pushed every envelope they could to make this conversation a reality. Two especially deserve mention. Even though I was the one to stand up in front of the crowd gathered from some seventeen states, it was Steve Monhollen who did most of the work leading up to the conference. And

Dean Daisy Machado pulled every administrative string she could to make sure Steve's work was successful.

But this was not a conversation made real only by support within the seminary walls. It was an ecumenical event that could not have occurred without the financial, prayerful, and hospitable support of a number of local churches in Lexington, Kentucky. Before the representatives of the New Homiletic met on a stage at the seminary on a Sunday afternoon, they stood separately in pulpits opened to them across the city. Thus, special thanks is to due to the following congregations and their pastors:

- Christ Church Cathedral, Morris K. Thompson Jr.
- Crestwood Christian Church (Disciples of Christ), William McDonald
- East Second Street Christian Church (Disciples of Christ), Donald K. Gillett II
- First United Methodist Church, J. Paul Brunstetter
- First Presbyterian Church, Lee W. Bowman

Thanks to Fortress Press, the 2007 conference was only the beginning of this conversation. I am grateful for their commitment to extending this dialogue to the wider public by publishing this book and DVD. I could not have hoped for a more positive response when I contacted colleagues in the homiletical guild asking them to be a part of this project. The higher level to which they have pushed the conversation is a gift I will cherish long after the pages of this volume have yellowed. As excited as I am about this conversation being published, I hate the idea of finishing this volume with them because I do not presently have another project pending with Fortress, which means I will not be working with David Lott. I hope this is only temporary, for he is a great editor and has been a supportive and challenging conversation partner across a number of projects I have worked on—all of which are better because he has worked on them.

My wife, Bonnie Cook, has rallied me on from the point of conceiving the conference to reviewing the final page proofs of this book. I am thankful that she has chosen to be my most intimate conversation partner throughout this project, throughout life.

Finally, I am most grateful to the primary conversation partners in this book. "Thanks" will hardly do. Even though their words fill up the bulk of the pages, on behalf of the seminary and the respondents, as well as preachers, homileticians, and churches across the land, I dedicate this book to David Buttrick, Fred Craddock, Gene Lowry, Henry Mitchell, and Charles Rice.

O. Wesley Allen Jr., editor

About the DVD

T he DVD included with this book holds video recordings of sermons by the five representatives of the New Homiletic that were all preached the same Sunday morning of The Re(New)ed Homiletic Conference in Lexington, Kentucky. Each was asked to offer a sermon that represented their rethinking of their own approach to proclamation. The sermons were preached at the following churches:

- ◆ David Buttrick
  First Presbyterian Church
- ◆ Fred B. Craddock
  Crestwood Christian Church
- ◆ Eugene L. Lowry
  First United Methodist Church
- ◆ Henry H. Mitchell
  East Second Street Christian Church
- ◆ Charles L. Rice
  Christ Church Cathedral

The Pillars of the New Homiletic
Back row, l to r: Charles L. Rice, Eugene L. Lowry, David Buttrick
Front row, l to r: Henry H. Mitchell, Fred B. Craddock

INTRODUCTION

The Pillars of the New Homiletic

O. Wesley Allen Jr.

W hether familiar with the label or not, preachers today take for granted the paradigm shift that has been called the New Homiletic. Forty years after its inception, the inductive, narrative, experiential approaches to proclamation that the New Homiletic introduced are common pulpit fare. While it may not seem all that new now, especially to those of us who were formed in the faith by this type of preaching, we should not forget that the movement breathed new life into an ailing pulpit. Amidst a host of writers, thinkers, and practitioners, Charles Rice, Fred Craddock, Henry Mitchell, Eugene Lowry, and David Buttrick are considered the pillars of this movement. Indeed, these scholars were first placed side by side in 1987 in a book by Richard L. Eslinger entitled *A New Hearing: Living Options in Homiletical Method.*[1] They gathered together again, this time in person, in 2007 (twenty years after the publication of *A New Hearing*) at Lexington Theological Seminary for a conference titled, similar to this book, *The Re(New)ed Homiletic.* As preachers and scholars struggle to imagine the most effective way to preach the gospel of Jesus Christ in the twenty-first century, it is important for us to hear again from these guides who helped us find a way through the homiletical wilderness in which the church found itself during the late twentieth century.

Each of the five scholar-preachers agreed to do three things in their presentations. First, he would rehearse the core contribution or perspective of his homiletical approach, focusing attention on what he thought was most important about his contribution. Second, he would describe his understanding of how the cultural, religious, theological, liturgical contexts have changed since he first developed that approach. And third (and primarily), he would name how he would reshape or nuance his core contribution for the future, given the shift(s) he had named. In addition to offering this lecture, engaging in question-and-answer time, and participating in a panel discussion with the other presenters, each scholar-preacher was asked to preach in a local congregation and offer a sermon that reflects their critique and reshaping of their early contribution to homiletics. This book offers to a wider public the lectures in essay form, two responses each from scholars indebted to their work that also look ahead to new trends in preaching, a closing essay by Eslinger, and videos of the sermons on the included DVD.

Before we turn to the re(new)ed thoughts of these scholar-preachers, an overview of the movement called the New Homiletic and an introduction to the work of these five pillars is in order. Their work, of course, did not occur in a vacuum. Thus, this introduction to the New Homiletic begins with some background work. I glance quickly at the dominant modes of preaching, over against which the New Homiletic spoke, and look at some (not all) of those whose work and thought served as a foundation for the New Homiletic to build on. I next offer an overview of the New Homiletic as a whole, followed by some comments on each scholar individually. Rather than an exhaustive or precise examination of either the history leading up to the New Homiletic or the work of these five pillars, what follows is an attempt to name key moments, figures, and concepts as a frame for entering the conversations that follow in this book.

Historical Background

In the later medieval period, the Franciscans and Dominicans developed a new form of preaching, usually referred to as the *university sermon*. One fifteenth-century preaching manuscript uses the metaphor of a tree to describe this new form.[2] From a very short trunk extends three major limbs, each of which bears three smaller branches. The approach is to take a central theme and break it into three points, each of which is then divided into three subsections. The university sermon was the beginning of the three-point, two-joke, and one-poem sermon. The approach is propositional: name the point or thesis at the beginning and break it into smaller didactic propositions for analysis. All jokes (and poems) aside, the endurance of this form shows that it has obviously served the church quite well for a long time.

Another sermonic form that has had lasting influence is the *Puritan Plain* style of preaching. Arising in late sixteenth-century Calvinism in England and New England, the form emphasizes less thematic preaching of three points and more exposition of Scripture. There are three major parts of the sermon—first, commentary on the ancient text in its ancient setting; second, eternal doctrinal points drawn from the exposition of the ancient text; and third, application of the doctrine to the current lives of those in the congregation—biblical exegesis, theological interpretation, moral exhortation. While the Puritan Plain form is different than the structure of the three-point sermon, the logic is the same. They are both deductive approaches to proclamation. They move from the general to the specific. In the Puritan Plain form, exegesis and theological reflection in the first parts of the sermon name general principles, which are then applied in specific ways at the end of the sermon.

These two homiletical forms together have dominated most of preaching in the West for the last four or five centuries. Even when the forms have not been held on to rigidly, the deductive logic and propositional approach to preaching they represent have been maintained. An example of this dominance is found in John A. Broadus's 1870 textbook *On the Preparation and Delivery of Sermons*. Revised by E. C. Dargan in 1897, by J. B. Weatherspoon in 1943, and again by Vernon L. Stanfield in 1979, some form of this book has been in print and in use for over a century. Indeed, it was *the* primary homiletical textbook used in seminaries from the late nineteenth century through the mid-twentieth century, especially the Weatherspoon edition. The influence of this textbook on American preaching is difficult to exaggerate. According to this text, a sermon should have a guiding subject that is named in the opening, often in the title itself. This subject should be argued persuasively, illustrated to make the abstract concrete and understandable, and applied so that the truth unpacked is given explicit relevance for life. In other words, Broadus, along with his revisers, taught students well how to preach deductive, propositional sermons.

Foundation

This traditional approach to preaching sat comfortably on its throne until the 1970s when the New Homiletic effected a *coup d'etat*. But while this was a radical dethronement, it was not as sudden as it often seems in hindsight. Throughout the twentieth century, there were some dissident voices among preachers that helped pave the way for the homiletical revolution of the 1970s and '80s. These voices, stacked upon one another, form the foundation upon which the pillars of the New Homiletic stand.

The first such voice I will mention is Harry Emerson Fosdick. Considered one of the greatest American preachers ever, this pastor of Riverside Church in New York City wrote an article for *Harper's Magazine* in 1928 entitled, "What Is the Matter with Preaching?"[3] Basically, he answered the question by saying the problem with most preaching is that it is boring. He rejected both expository and topical preaching for falling into this problem. One of his long-remembered lines from the article is, "Only the preacher proceeds upon the idea that folk come to church desperately anxious to discover what happened to the Jebusites." Fosdick argued instead that sermons should solve problems of the hearers—some social, moral, psychological, theological, existential problem of importance. If preaching truly touches hearers' lives, it will be anything but boring. By starting with people's needs, sermons will be relevant and transforming. While the New Homiletic did not necessarily embrace Fosdick's psychological emphasis, it did make a turn to the hearer that has similar dynamics.

Another homiletical voice that foreshadowed elements of the New Homiletic was that of R. E. C. Browne. In 1958, Browne published *Ministry of the*

Word, in which he argues that the gospel should not be reduced to formulae, by which he means predetermined propositions and structures of sermons (such as three-point or expository forms).[4] Instead, the sermon must authentically and artistically grow out of the character of the person preaching and relate to the form of revelation represented in the biblical text being preached. Preaching should be more artistic poetry than philosophical prose.

1958 was a good year for homiletics as H. Grady Davis's even more influential *Design for Preaching* appeared alongside Browne's work.[5] Davis's opening words of the book are, "Life appears in the union of substance and form."[6] Davis could not understand why preachers took every aspect of the gospel and forced it to conform to a single rhetorical form, such as the three-point sermon. Instead, he argued, "there is a right form for each sermon, namely, the form that is right for this particular sermon."[7] Sermonic form and content should be organically related. "A sermon should be like a tree," he says, but this is a different sort of tree than the medieval preaching tree we considered earlier. A sermon should have one sturdy idea like the trunk, deep roots of research and reflection that are never seen, branches that thrust out from the central trunk that bear fruit, and blossoms appropriate to that tree alone.[8] So, the sermon's content determines the appropriate form, rather than the form determining how the content must be presented.

Fosdick, Browne, and Davis foreshadowed the New Homiletic by raising significant questions about the overall effectiveness of the dominant homiletical paradigm. They are some of the homileticians upon whose shoulders Buttrick, Craddock, Lowry, Mitchell, and Rice stood.

But, actually, there were some stronger forces of change occurring in other academic disciplines that would undergird the rise of the New Homiletic. A beginning point in the first half of the twentieth century has been labeled the *linguistic turn*. Ludwig Wittgenstein, Martin Heidegger, and others began to assert in different ways that language does not simply name reality; language *constructs* reality. The power of this insight for preaching is easily imagined in Heidegger's famous line, "Language is the house of Being."[9]

In the mid-twentieth century, New Testament scholar Rudolf Bultmann applied Heidegger's existentialist philosophy to biblical hermeneutics.[10] He used existentialism to translate the myths of the ancient biblical worldview into relevant theological discourse in a modern, scientific worldview. Two of Bultmann's students, Ernst Fuchs and Gerhard Ebeling, extended both his ideas and Heidegger's later work on the power of language into a school of thought referred to as the New Hermeneutic in the 1960s.[11] Instead of approaching Scripture as history or as a collection of eternal truths, or even as myths to be demythologized, they viewed Scripture as *word event*. Language does not simply refer; it acts, it does, it is an event that creates meaning and meaningfulness. Over against the approach of earlier historical critics who tried to study Scripture in a scientific, objective, distant manner, the New Hermeneutic argues that proper interpretation of Scripture requires that one be existentially invested to allow the Word to act upon you. Not only do interpreters ask questions of the text, the text asks questions of the interpreter. To read Scripture as a depository of content misses the point. To read Scripture truly is to have an experience of, an encounter with, the Word of God which demands that the reader make a decision for authentic existence. Moreover, because Scripture is at root *kerygma* (proclamation), preaching should do what Scripture does. That is, instead of simply passing on the content of the faith persuasively, preaching should be an *event* that leads the hearer into an encounter with the Word of God which calls for transformative decisions.

At the same time that the New Hermeneutic was taking hold in New Testament theology in North America, biblical scholars and theologians moved out of the history department and instead began sharing office space with the English department. That is not to say that a complete either-or was set up—either the Bible is read as history or as literature—but it was a major shift nevertheless. In the 1960s and '70s, literary-critical readings of the Bible began to surpass historical-critical readings. Biblical scholars like Amos Wilder, brother of playwright and novelist Thornton Wilder, led the charge in analyzing Scripture as narrative.[12] A growing appreciation of the literary-narrative quality of Scripture led those in the New Homiletic to a new appreciation of the essential role of narrative and literary art in preaching.

One final, related yet distinct movement that played a role in the shaping of the New Homiletic was the arena of cultural studies distinguishing between oral and print cultures. Two of the most influential voices of the day were Marshal McLuhan and Walter Ong.[13] One of the central things they argued is that logic works differently in different media. Knowledge is shaped by how it is conveyed—or, to use McLuhan's famous line, "The medium is the message." The implications for preaching are obvious. We should not preach using the same kind of argumentation we use when writing. The dominant deductive, propositional approach to preaching was shaped by print logic. Different approaches are called for in oral discourse.

These different homiletical and scholarly voices came together in the 1960s and '70s when cultural forces were leading many people to challenge the authority of the church and the relevancy of preaching. The result was a homiletical tipping point. The time was ripe for a change in the way North American preachers went about the task of proclaiming the gospel of Jesus Christ. This came about in the 1970s and '80s in the New Homiletic. But we need to be careful not to exaggerate this claim concerning a tipping point in a way that diminishes the innovation of the pillars of the New Homiletic. These scholar-preachers did not simply ride the wave of the time. They did not simply summarize what had already been said in a new way. Instead, they stood up, stood out, and spoke out—a right word at the right time.

The New Homiletic

So we turn now to that paradigm shift called the New Homiletic. Before we look specifically at Rice, Craddock, Mitchell, Lowry, and Buttrick, there are some things we can say about the movement as a whole, that is, by the way, broader than just the proposal of these five men.

David James Randolph was teaching homiletics at Drew School of Theology in 1965 when he delivered a paper at the first meeting of the Academy of Homiletics and coined the term *New Homiletic*. He saw this nascent, new preaching as an outgrowth of the New Hermeneutic (thus the linguistic echo), but not that alone. He wrote,

> A new preaching is coming to birth in the travail of our times. In the civil rights movement, in the engagement with communism, in the "secular city," in the ecumenical enterprise, in the theological school, in the parish church, in the liturgical movement, and elsewhere, preaching is being rejected as a habit and affirmed as a happening. The definition of preaching which is dawning on these horizons may

be stated in this way: Preaching is the event in which the biblical text is interpreted in order that its meaning will come to expression in the concrete situation of the hearers.[14]

Randolph's use of the label *New Homiletic* was proleptic. What would come over the horizon was not quite clear yet. But now looking back over the past thirty-five to forty years we can list some common elements of the shift in preaching that occurred in the 1970s and '80s. The characteristics I am going to list are common denominators, if you will, and are meant to be illustrative more than exhaustive. Moreover, they overlap in a messy sort of way. For the pure irony of it, I offer this description using three points!

First, the New Homiletic represented a turn to the hearer. Earlier homiletical works usually focused on how the preacher builds an argument. The New Homiletic focused instead on how people in the pew listen, how they experience spoken language. Instead of constructing language simply to serve the content, you play with language to invite hearers to *experience* something specific. In classical rhetorical terms, there is shift in emphasis from logos to pathos. We must be careful not to hear this shift as saying preachers should have no concern for content. The question is not whether or not a sermon should be theological or biblical, but *how* a theologically, biblically informed worldview should be offered so that it creates a transformative, authentic experience for the hearers.

Indeed, this approach assumes the hearer is a partner in the sermonic event. What preachers offer is only the start of the sermon. Those in the pew must finish the work. To draw every sermon up nice and neat is to refuse the hearers their due. They must have the freedom to assent or disagree with what is proclaimed, or it is not good news. They must be able to "apply" the word spoken to their own lives in their own ways without it being dictated, or there is no freedom.

Second, to enable hearers to do their sermonic work appropriately, there must be a shift in how sermons are offered. It is not overly dramatic to call this paradigm shift a homiletical revolution. After four to five hundred years of deductive sermons, the New Homiletic said, "No more." In their place were offered inductive, narrative-type sermons. Whereas deductive sermons move from general claims to specific applications for the lives of those in the congregation, sermons in the new mode move from the specifics of lived experience to general claims. As we are experientially moved along with the plot of a great short story or movie, so must sermons move us. There must be suspense or tension in the early part of the sermon that leads the hearer to seek resolution, both in the sermon and in existence. After all, as we just noted, this is the hearers' work.

This means, then, that sermons in the vein of the New Homiletic are expressed in the indicative instead of the imperative. Deductive sermons generally move from exposition of Scripture or doctrine to moral application. Preachers authoritatively tell you how to live as a Christian. Inductive or narrative sermons empower and authorize the hearer to do the work of application. The tools the preacher gives to those in the pew to hear God's call is an evocative declaration of God's good news. The preacher speaks of what is so that hearers are moved to decide what will be.

Third, in the wake of the linguistic turn in philosophy and the New Hermeneutic, preachers view sermonic language differently from their predecessors. Propositional sermons work on the assumption that language is a clear, precise tool to convey truth. Thus, the main elements of the sermon are the abstract, theological, moral points. Imagery is used to "illustrate" these main points, to make them more concrete, more palatable. Illustrations are add-ons that are helpful to "bring home" the message, but the message itself would not change if they were omitted. For the New Homiletic, however, the imagery *is* the message. For this movement, sermonic content is not propositional truth but a true, existential, transformative experience of the good news. The sermon, like Scripture itself, is a word *event*. The language shapes not simply human beliefs (which is the orientation of propositional sermons), but human perception and experience—in a nutshell, human reality. So, figurative language, metaphors, and stories are not rhetorical flourishes in sermons; they are what bring into being a new consciousness of the hearers. They do not simply show hearers reality; they initiate the congregation into the really real, the ultimately real.

So the shift represented by the New Homiletic can be summarized in terms of a focus on the hearer, the use of inductive, narrative sermonic forms, and the centrality of imagistic, storied language to create an experience of the gospel. But lest we be reductionistic, we need to recognize that different scholars grouped under the umbrella of the New Homiletic approach the core values in different ways. They are influenced by different strands of the background described above, and each has a variety of other influences as well. So while their homiletic journeys brought them all into the same neighborhood, they came by different roads and settled down on different streets. Let's examine them in the order they appeared in the neighborhood.

Charles L. Rice

Charles L. Rice began life as a Southern Baptist, migrated through the United Church of Christ, and settled down in the Episcopal Church. He spent over thirty years teaching at Drew School of Theology in Madison, New Jersey, where he taught both M.Div. and Ph.D. students.

In 1970, Rice published *Interpretation and Imagination: The Preacher and Contemporary Literature*.[15] Here he begins with Paul Tillich's dictum that religion is the substance of culture, and culture is the form of religion. Thus, biblical preaching consists of translating the faith from an ancient language system into a contemporary cultural language system.

To capture the essence of the faith in terms of contemporary cultural experience, one must first bring contemporary human experience to bear on biblical interpretation. Rice argues, in similar fashion to Tillich, that the best expression of contemporary culture is found in contemporary art. Artists have always both caught the essence of human experience and redefined human experience. Thus, preachers are well served by colliding contemporary literature with ancient biblical literature. This is more than simply drawing illustrations from literature, as preachers have always done. The preacher seeks a sort of resonance between the experience found in the ancient text and in the contemporary text; by letting the texts rub together, the hearers are offered that same-type experience in their own cultural terms while affirming the historic tradition of the faith.

In 1980 Rice coauthored a textbook with Edmund Steimle and Morris Neidenthal entitled *Preaching the Story*.[16] In the long run, this book was more influential than *Interpretation and Imagination*, but it is clearly an extension of Rice's earlier argument. In this book, the authors assert that the task of the preacher is to bring together in the sermon—in a way that is meaningful to the hearers and faithful to the tradition—the biblical story, the congregation's story, the preacher's personal story, and the world's story.

A key exegetical and homiletical principle for this approach is that *story interprets story*. In this sense, preaching itself *is* storytelling. It is not, however, just stringing together entertaining illustrations. It is the laying bare of these four stories side by side, overlapping their edges, so that at times they sing together in harmony and at other times they enter into a shouting match filled with dissonance, but they always interpret each other and those gathered for worship.

Henry H. Mitchell

Henry H. Mitchell stands in a long line of vibrant African American preachers. Both of his grandfathers were preachers, but when he looks backward his vision stretches all the way to Africa. While he is a child of black preaching, he is the father of African American homiletics. Published in 1970—and thus developed at the same time Rice was composing his work—*Black Preaching* was a groundbreaking study.[17] Some (white) scholars disparaged black preaching as uneducated or filled with emotionalism, and others tried to deny that there was anything really unique about black preaching when compared with European American preaching. But Mitchell lifted up this preaching style, which had its origin in the African griot and took shape during the struggle to survive in slavery, as something for the African American preacher to be proud of and something for all preachers to learn from. Indeed, in 1977 he published a book that grew out of his 1974 Lyman Beecher lectures, entitled *The Recovery of Preaching*.[18] This book shifts from description to prescription, while continuing to use elements from black preaching as its basis. Like Rice and Craddock, he argues that preachers must speak to the culture in which the congregation resides and speak out of their own personal lives. But a unique theme of his work is that good preaching involves celebration. Rejecting the Western dualism of intellect and emotion that results in rational, propositional sermons, he argues that preachers must engage the whole person. If we are commanded to love God with our whole heart, soul, strength, and mind, preachers cannot only address the mind. African Americans, he asserts, had spent centuries having tapes recorded in their heads telling them they are inferior, subhuman, and loved less by God than whites. Preaching must erase such tapes and record new messages on hearers' souls. You do not do this with argumentation.

You must move hearers emotionally to embrace new images of God and self through storytelling, folk language, and evocative imagery.

Key to this transformation is the climax of the African American sermon. For Mitchell, the climax must be celebratory.[19] The preacher must celebrate and lead the congregation in celebration of God's sovereignty. For the black church to celebrate God's eschatological goodness in worship in the face of slavery, Jim Crow laws, segregation, and continued economic discrimination is an amazing Christian witness. And it is transforming for those who join in the celebration. Worshipers cannot celebrate God's sovereignty and at the same despair that evil will have the last word in their lives or in the world. Thus, celebration leads to new faith, which leads to new action.

Fred B. Craddock

Fred B. Craddock actually wrote and published locally at Philips University *As One without Authority* before Charles Rice published *Interpretation and Imagination*. But it was a year later before it was published nationally.[20] In other words, Craddock's, Rice's, and Mitchell's thoughts were developed simultaneously. In terms of public influence, Rice's book started a nice fall shower and Craddock's book grew that shower into a thunderous spring storm. Indeed, many consider *As One without Authority* to be the most influential book on preaching in the last half century.

In 1978, Craddock published the Lyman Beecher lectures he gave at Yale under the title *Overhearing the Gospel: Preaching and Teaching the Faith to Those Who Have Already Heard.*[21] In this book he applies the argument in *As One without Authority* to the task of preaching to those for whom the gospel has grown dull through familiarity. As he draws on Søren Kierkegaard indirectly in the first volume, he does so explicitly in the second.

In *As One without Authority*, Craddock asks, If deductive preaching is not really working anymore, why not try an inductive approach? In 1971 this was a radical proposal. Preachers were so used to moving from a general truth claim to particular applications that many assumed it was essential to proclamation. You state a proposition drawn from the gospel and then you tell people what it means for their lives. But drawing on the New Hermeneutic and the literary study of Jesus' parables, Craddock asserts that preaching should instead move from the particulars of experience to general truth. Notice that the language of application is dropped. Craddock pulls back the authority of the preacher from exhorting the hearers how to live their lives. If, he argues, the inductive process is done well, hearers will be led to finish the sermon by drawing the conclusion for themselves and determining how it should be applied to their particular lives. Hearers are participants in the sermon event, not simply recipients of it. The hearers are able to do their part in finishing the sermon because the preacher has provided a range of concrete experiential images with which they can relate and draw analogies to their own existence. You show them their lives in light of the gospel and they will do something with it.

In the study, the preacher works with a text and through the encounter with the biblical text gains new insight into God, self, and the world. This is not simply an intellectual process; it is emotional, experiential. The preacher's task is to recreate that experience for the hearers. But the preacher cannot do this by reporting what she has found anymore than showing someone pictures of a vacation is equal to taking them on vacation. But that is what deductive sermons try to do. Rather, the preacher must lead the congregation in a process of discovery appropriate to the oral setting of worship. So, through study of the text the preacher decides where she wants the congregation to be at the end of the sermon. Through study of the congregation, she determines where the hearers are at the moment. Sermons then take the listeners on a journey from where they exist to a vision and experience of something new.

The vehicle that takes them on the journey is imagery. Inductive preachers drive the congregation through the familiar roads of their lives in a way that they can see and experience the landscape anew through the lens of the gospel. To change people you do not tell them the images stuck in their heads are wrong; you offer them new images. So, sermonic imagery is not simply illustrative of things said more directly in propositional form. Imagination is the way to a new reality.

Eugene L. Lowry

Eugene L. Lowry's work is in some way an extension of the trajectories that began with Charles Rice and Fred Craddock. In his 1980 book, *The*

Homiletical Plot, Lowry takes inductive movement and storytelling and shapes it into a concrete sermonic form.[22] He argues that all sermons should take on a narrative structure. This is not to say that every sermon should be a story, but that, like all narratives, the sermon must move from conflict to resolution, or from itch to scratch. The specific construct he uses to unpack this narrative structure has become known as the Lowry Loop.

The narrative movement has five stages. The first move is to create the itch for the hearers the way a narrative does—to get them engaged by developing some ambiguity that will need to be resolved. Lowry calls this upsetting the equilibrium.

The second stage involves digging deeper into ambiguity to determine all that is really at stake. Here the preacher and congregation analyze the discrepancy between what is and what can or ought to be. This stage asks a slow, thoughtful *Why?* in the face of the itch created at the beginning of the sermon.

All narratives to some degree move toward an ending that resolves the conflict created earlier in the story. The third stage of a narrative sermon, therefore, discloses the clue to that resolution without giving it away all at once. To be effective, the preacher must offer the congregation an experience of reversal at this point. There must be an "Oh, I get it."

This revelatory moment in the sermon leads the hearers to an experience in which the radical discontinuity between the world's way of thinking and the gospel is seen and felt. So in the fourth stage of the narrative sermon, Lowry moves us from diagnosis to treatment. Here listeners hear the good news proclaimed explicitly and find that the gospel is continuous with human experience as long as human experience has been turned upside down.

The final stage of the narrative sermon that flows out of experiencing the gospel in the sermon is the anticipation of the consequences of embracing the gospel in the future—once the speaking of the sermon is done. In the sermon itself, treatment has only begun, it has only made health a possibility. The hearers must decide for themselves what difference the gospel will make in their lives. In this final stage the preacher does not exhort the congregation to live out the gospel in a specific way, but invites authentic response.

These are the five stages of the Lowry Loop, but the language is a little cumbersome, so Lowry gives us shorthand terms: Oops!, Ugh!, Aha!, Whee!, and Yeah!

David Buttrick

While David Buttrick clearly fits within the New Homiletic in terms of the common characteristics named earlier, he often comes at those concerns from quite different angles than these other four scholars. He is as different from the other four as he is similar. Buttrick had been developing and discussing his ideas in short works in the early 1980s and then published *Homiletic: Moves and Structures* as his magnum opus in 1987 (after Eslinger had already included his approach alongside that of the other four).[23] To give you a sense of the scope of the work by way of comparison, in its original format, Lowry's *Homiletical Plot* was one hundred pages long, while Buttrick's *Homiletic* is 498 pages. Whereas the other works we have been discussing present a singular theoretical perspective, Buttrick presents two key theoretical pieces mixed in with a plethora of theological observations and homiletical advice.

Buttrick's starting point is the same as all the others: he rejects the dominant homiletical approach of distilling propositions from Scripture regardless of the form of the text. He desires a homiletical method that better reflects the literary study of the Bible, especially the recognition that biblical narratives are movements of episodic thought. By plotting the underlying structure of thought in a biblical passage (in a fashion similar to but not quite the same as structuralism), a preacher can see the way the text intends to function in the reader's consciousness and develop a sermon that functions in the same way in the congregation's consciousness. The connective logic of the sermon should reflect the function of the movement of the biblical text on which the sermon is focused.

Indeed, coupled with this hermeneutical concern is one that a homiletical approach must fit the way people listen today. At the center of Buttrick's homiletical approach is an empirical, phenomenological examination of the manner in which language forms in communal consciousness. While all of the scholars we have examined make a turn toward the individual hearer, Buttrick, based on insights drawn from communication studies, focuses on how a *community* of listeners can be moved along to hear the same sermon in the same basic way. The complex details of Buttrick's argument can be controversial and difficult to follow, but his basic method is straightforward: determine the way thought forms in a community's mind and develop a sermonic structure that flows in that same manner.

The subtitle of the book names the two primary ways the preacher can create such a communal hearing. The two parts are not unrelated, but they are separate. The first part focuses on sermonic "moves." Buttrick rejects the use of "points" but is very much interested in the way sermons offer the congregation a number of ideas, or language modules. These ideas are not static but are movements of thought similar to the way different ideas move through a conversation. A conversation between two people moves with a rapid exchange of shifting ideas. But a sermonic conversation with a community of hearers must move much more slowly and deliberately and shift between ideas more carefully. Modern attention span is limited to three to four minutes, but it takes three to four minutes to embed a movement of thought in a whole community's consciousness. So the preacher must shape a move very carefully. The move should open with a statement of the idea. Actually, the idea should be stated three times, but the repetition is formed differently each time so that the community is not aware of the repetition, even as it begins to embed the idea in the community's consciousness. Then the idea is developed through association or dissociation through the use of a central image. Finally, closure is brought to the move through the restatement of the idea. This sandwich structure allows the hearers to understand, assimilate, and remember the move as the preacher shifts to the next move.

Different from Craddock's journey or Lowry's narrative plot, Buttrick does not think the preacher should develop smooth transitions between these moves so much as keeping them separate by placing them side by side in progression so that the logical connection between the ideas is clear. During twenty minutes, you can develop a five- or six-move sermon.

While the moves are set apart from each other in the way that they are opened and closed, they must work together. One of the ways they do this is through the interrelationship of the sermonic imagery. Instead of simply illustrating propositions, the central imagery of each of the conjoined moves should work together to form an "image grid" that reinforces the central claim of the sermon and embeds it in the hearers' consciousness. Because abstract, conceptual language no longer forms in group consciousness as it did in a pretechnology age, the use of story and metaphor becomes central to homiletical endeavor instead of an illustrative add-on. However, the wrong image can split communal consciousness instead of forming in consciousness. For example, Buttrick absolutely rejects the use of personal stories in sermons because they draw the audience's attention away conceptual development intended and place it on the person of the preacher. The image grid constructed by the preacher stretches across the episodic plot of the sermon through the careful placement of moves to make a specific impression on the congregation.

The second half of *Homiletic* focuses on "structures," by which Buttrick means overarching rhetorical strategies aimed at different sermonic intentions. This section of the book has been overshadowed by the influence of the moves section, so we need not give it the same level of attention, but at least a brief summary is needed.

Buttrick suggests that the connective logic of moves should aim toward one of three modes of impressions in congregational consciousness. These three modes are like different responses to a painting of city scene in a museum.

The first is the *immediacy mode*; it is like the first glance at the painting and the immediate impression it makes on you. Sermons in this mode might be structured to duplicate the structure of biblical narrative to offer an immediate experiential impression.

The second mode is the *reflection mode*; it is like returning to the painting later and sitting on the bench in the room and really studying the details of the city scene. Sermons in this mode back away from the immediate surface-level impression of a biblical passage and reflect on the more slowly developed meaning of a passage. This sermon would deal more explicitly with theology than the former.

And finally there is the *praxis mode*. This is like leaving the museum with the image of the painting in the back of your mind and seeing the city outside the museum in a new light. Sermons in this mode begin less with the biblical text and more with the situation facing the congregation. They analyze what congregations are doing and speak to what a congregation *should* do.

Conclusion

These are the early works of the five pillars of the New Homiletic—Charles Rice, Fred Craddock, Henry Mitchell, Eugene Lowry, and David Buttrick.

Their core contributions continue to be influential in preaching and the study of preaching today. There are few preachers whose approach has not been shaped directly or indirectly by them. There are no homileticians teaching in North America today who would not name this group as the shoulders upon which we stand.

But that said, the movement had its roots in the 1960s, sprouted in the 1970s, and matured in the 1980s. Given that the movement has been around for nearly forty years, given the rise of postmodernity, and given the decline of the mainline church, the New Homiletic is experiencing a midlife crisis of sorts. Many people are looking for the next major move in preaching. But if the current homiletical literature is an appropriate measure, it is not likely that such a move will be an abandonment of the New Homiletic so much as it will be an extension and adaptation of it. So it only makes sense that these five pillars have a chance to give voice to their vision for how that should happen alongside all of us young whippersnapper homileticians trying to find our way in the dark.

When one looks at this group of five scholars, one is likely immediately aware that they are all men and four of them are white. The homiletical guild has diversified significantly since the 1970s and '80s, and the preaching landscape promises to change even more radically in the coming years. Thus, we have created an intergenerational dialogue of sorts in this volume by inviting a range of homileticians who are planting seeds here in the early part of the twenty-first century for harvest in the coming years to respond to the re(new)ed proposals of the New Homileticians. In addition, we offer an afterword from Richard Eslinger, who was the first to bring these pillars together in a single study.

1

Storytelling Renewed

Charles L. Rice

School Days

In the late 1950s, the earliest theological influence on my fledgling preaching came from Karl Barth, by way of a young professor at Baylor who had spent a sabbatical with Barth. Dr. David Mueller came back from Europe to tell us that preaching was about the text, the whole text, and nothing but the text. As a result, I treated my little country church—not far from George W. Bush's ranch in the hill country of Texas—to a yearlong exposition, verse by dogged verse, of the epistle to the Romans. In the early '60s, while at the seminary in Louisville, I majored in New Testament and stuck pretty much to Barth's homiletic.

America changed in the 1960s, no less for preachers than for everyone else. The place of the church in society, the relevance of religion to the wrenching events of the day, the authority of leaders—none of that could be taken for granted. Many—both inside and outside the churches, and even in the seminaries—were not so sure that the preacher was any longer a player to be taken seriously. One semester in the late '60s, at Union Theological Seminary in New York, Edmund Steimle—distinguished professor of homiletics and a giant among preachers—had no students. Students were mounting the barricades, just as the church and its theologians were seeking relevance, if not validation, in relation to the issues and crusades of the day. It was in this period that courses in preaching and books on homiletics began to choose titles that connected preaching to other fields and to pressing issues of the day.

By 1970, when my first book was published and I began teaching at Drew, I had been preaching for a dozen years as a student pastor in Texas and Kentucky. The year in New York (studying with Steimle at Union), followed by doctoral study at Duke (where I taught the 8 A.M. preaching labs for four years!) had alerted me to the changing status of preaching. The image of the preacher in my grandparents' church, and in those country charges of mine—the awesome man opening the big book, putting his finger on the text, and speaking to us in tones befitting the Word of God—seemed no longer quite viable.

That first book, the last in "The Preacher's Paperback Library" series, was one of those *and* books: *Interpretation and Imagination: The Preacher and Contemporary Literature*. My career as a preacher and teacher of preachers has unfolded along the lines of those beginnings—as a dialogue with culture, as self-expressive communication, and as storytelling.

Preaching in Dialogue with Culture. Professor Steimle, in his course on doctrinal preaching, assigned sermons on four doctrines for the fall semester in 1963. We were to think theologically about each doctrine—in my case, the priesthood of all believers, grace, the second coming of Christ, and the last judgment—and then we were to speak as nontheologically as possible. While working on that, I was in a course with Roger Shinn, "Christian Faith and Existentialist Literature." A dialogue began in me, between William Faulkner and the Revelation of John of Patmos. That led to Saul Bellow, the movies, and an obscure poem about the streets of New York. In the beginning, there may have been an undue dependence upon the popular arts for something relevant or interesting to say in the pulpit. But with the help of Tillich's theology of culture, the work of Frederick Buechner and Amos Wilder, and especially the biblical reorientation provided by Fred Craddock, the dialogue with culture became more faithful. I began to see more clearly the broader meaning of Steimle's dictum in his November 1966 James Gray lectures at Duke University: "The sermon that starts in the Bible and stays in the Bible is not biblical." Preaching is always, by its very nature, in dialogue with culture.

Preaching as Self-Expression. While in my first semester at Drew Theological School as a young scholar, Steimle asked me to give a paper at the Academy of Homiletics meeting in Princeton. I could hardly have been more nervous. We met in an elegant room where Dr. Steimle sat on one side of the fireplace and Professor Donald McLeod on the other, both in wingback chairs, as I stood with my back to the fire! I felt out of my league. But some preppy clothes from Brooks Brothers helped me look the part of a scholar, and an incident in my very first class provided me with material on which to reflect for the lecture.

The incident was this: in that first class at Drew I had heard a polished, biblical sermon that modeled sound preaching techniques of the day, but it seemed to have had little effect on the hearers. Right afterward, I heard a less obviously scriptural, but highly confessional, deeply human homily—given by my first female student. It not only connected well with the coming season of Advent, it also connected with the class on that dark November day. I used this incident to help me formulate my thinking about the expressive aspect called for in preaching.[1]

Joseph Sittler became the theologian for this expressive aspect of my work. He asserts, "Preaching is not merely something a preacher does; it is a function of the preacher's whole existence concentrated at the point of declaration and interpretation. The act of preaching is organic to the placement of the person (*man himself*) [sic] as believer, doubter, sinner, aspirer . . ."[2] I would eventually connect this concern for self-expression in the pulpit with ecclesiology and an understanding of liturgy and priesthood in my 1991 book *The Embodied Word*.[3]

Preaching as Story. In 1980, Steimle, Morris Niedenthal, and I published *Preaching the Story* to show the organic relation of preaching to the stories of Scripture, the preacher, the congregation and its liturgy, and the culture. That book presupposes that the Bible itself is best understood as an unfolding, overarching story comprising many diverse stories. Imagination is essential to exegesis and proclamation; one hears most clearly, most deeply, when listening with the ears of a wondering child. Preaching depends profoundly on the right brain, as in storytelling. We can trust the story—as Jesus so obviously did in his parables—to discover and tease out the ways of God. The story is not afraid of irony, contradiction, ambiguity, or playfulness. The arena of the story is this world, while its agenda reaches beyond the obvious and conventional. A good story always has the possibility of telling more than first meets the ear, and there lies the essential, ironic connection between the earthy, recognizably human story and the Word made flesh.

Preaching as Liturgy. A fourth theme that emerged halfway through my career is preaching *as* liturgy. It seems important to put it that way, not preaching *and* liturgy. The Word of God occurs as an event in time, and preaching is one movement integral to the whole. Preaching is impossible outside the people's work, illumined and empowered by the liturgical assembly, its language, and action.

Vatican II and the subsequent new books of worship in the various denominations reshaped and enriched the liturgical context of preaching. The importance of this became clear to me through my experience as a teacher—students exhibited the disconnect between sermon and liturgy—and through a month's stay at Taizé as part of a 1984 sabbatical. Looking for a place where the Word was spoken at the table, I joined an early Thursday morning Eucharist at the parish nearest Drew. This became the center of my spiritual life and the model for my teaching, leading to a new course at the Theological School, "The Church at Worship", that comprised church music, liturgy, and preaching, and to the publication of *The Embodied Word*. That book calls for preaching at the table with the baptistery clearly in view.

Forty Years Later

For forty years now the Academy of Homiletics has been meeting in early Advent, working on preaching in relation to exegesis, hermeneutics, pedagogy, social issues, worship, theology, the arts, ecclesiology, and so on. The context of that work has been a constantly and rapidly changing culture, to which homiletics—like a canary in a volatile mine—has been particularly sensitive. It would be hard to come up with a field of study that by its very nature is so responsive to cultural change. For many semesters at Drew I taught a course called "Contemporary Preaching," an embarrassingly redundant title coming from a preacher who cannot watch the news, go to a movie, or read the paper without Sunday morning coming into view.

So, from one preacher's point of view, what shifts have we seen—some seismic, some slow and subtle but relentless—that reshape our homiletic? Forty years have brought changes not only to this vast and diverse country, but new links being forged every day between the economies, cultures, and religions of the world. Four categories, which inevitably overlap, provide a means of getting at so large a topic.

American Culture. For most people, especially those looking on from the outside, the tendency of American culture is toward wealth, consuming, entertainment, technology, personal—especially sexual—freedom, military power, diversity, and religiosity. As the largest transfer of wealth in the history of humankind is now occurring—the baby boomers beginning to pass their wealth on to their progeny, some thirty trillion dollars—the gap widens between haves and have-nots. The technological revolution in communication widens the distance between generations, the sexual revolution splits denominations, and religion coupled with politics polarizes the nation as it paralyzes politics. Electronic communication—from television to the Internet—has diminished interest in association (whether in bowling leagues or congregations), exacerbating historic American individualism. As the screen replaces the book, and Hollywood's production neither displays nor demands poetic, ironic engagement, we see the decline of the active imagination. The implications of this for the spoken word in general and for the possibilities of preaching remain to be seen.

American Religion. Americans remain—certainly in comparison to the industrialized world—very religious. But, increasingly, this does not mean attachment to a denomination or to a congregation. Many prefer "spirituality"—*vaporized* religion, Flannery O'Connor called it—to the idea of practicing a particular religion. The historical roots of Christianity have been loosened, and the tendency is toward a more free-floating religiosity, sometimes institutionalized in the so-called megachurch. There is much less commonality of religious practice than half a century ago. As seen in Ken Burns's marathon documentary *The War*, on that Sunday morning of December 7, 1941, just about everyone was getting ready to go to Sunday school. President Roosevelt prayed with the nation as if they were all in church together. As late as the 1950s most of us read from the King James Bible in church and Sunday school. Today's preacher cannot assume— even in the gathered congregation on Sunday morning—common religious experience, attachment to a denomination or even to historic Christianity, or shared knowledge of or consent to the Bible.

American Theology. Two significant theological developments stand out. First, there is the resurgence of fundamentalism. Judaism and Islam are affected, and in American Christianity the tight theological system and closed mind of fundamentalism is widespread and found across denominations. Second, we see the decline of the authoritative theological voice as it is replaced by popular theology. This skepticism of authority, grounded in relativism and modern suspicion, questions all claims to possess and speak the truth. This would be somewhat analogous to the phenomenal rise of YouTube and other forms of electronic communication focused on personal experience and opinion rather than on any claim to academic authority or intellectual credentials. The convinced zealot quoting Scripture or the relativistic cynic can be a formidable auditor, not to be swayed by tradition, theologians, or even appeals to reason or human experience.

American Worship. There has been a considerable shift in the idea of *church* in America. Yngve Brilioth, a historian of preaching, once said that if there is anything we can say for sure about liturgy in America it is that there are no "liturgical fetters."[4] Recent experience bears that out. In music, architecture, liturgical symbols and forms, styles of preaching, churchly manners— anything goes. In some places the preacher cannot be sure that there will be a pulpit in the church! Large, popular churches avoid historic liturgical symbols, intent upon making the congregation comfortable and minimizing the unfamiliar or challenging.

Vatican II brought liturgical reform to most mainline denominations, and the Eucharist occupies a larger place in many congregations, but the integration of Word and sacrament remains incomplete. It may be fair to say that in the larger churches an entrepreneurial spirit—the need to fill the pews and subscribe a budget to support sound and light, multiple programs, and corporate-like staffs—can shape both liturgy and preaching.

Ecclesiology and liturgical theology continue to be marginalized, their pertinence to the present situation notwithstanding. For my own approach to preaching—formed in the '60s—these four cultural shifts raise questions as to the content, form, and style of preaching today. In some cases, a homiletical approach long in the making would seem to meet today's situation. Other aspects of a dialogical, self-expressive, storytelling homiletic may call for critique and renovation.

Renovation

I find myself surprisingly close to where I started, in fact, to a gospel hymn that my Baptist grandmother liked to sing in her kitchen:

> Tell me the story of Jesus,
> write on my heart every word.
> Tell me the story most precious,
> sweetest that ever was heard.

To be more postmodern, we might change the last line, "Sweetest that ever *I've* heard." Be that as it may, what we hope for is to keep on telling this story, to ourselves and others, in such a way that it comes alive in our community, gathering weekly to hear it, living daily in it, alive to each other and to God.

Every month or so my partner and I drive down to hear the Philadelphia Symphony Orchestra. We have had the same seats, next to an older couple, for several years. They seem to enjoy the music, most of which they have heard before. It happened again this year. The woman was wearing her opening-night red dress and a flower in her hair. After they were settled, before opening her program, she looked all around as the orchestra tuned up and Verizon Hall filled. With unabashed excitement she said to her husband, "Oh, isn't this wonderful! Just look at these seats!" To which he patiently replied, "You sit here every year." It is something like what happened to that woman in the red dress that every preacher must hope and pray for.

Our house in the Delaware River Valley was built by German farmers two hundred years ago. One carpenter helping us with restoration said, "We should stop this project, tear this house down, cut every timber and board in two, and build two houses." It is that kind of house: solid, showing the marks of human labor and care, with a lot of living seeping from plaster walls and squeaky floors. It is a good, and challenging, place to live. In the same way, looking back over forty years of preaching, it appears that much remains of the earliest structure, elements that may simply be essential to preaching: tradition in dialogue with culture, a person speaking, and the telling and retelling of a community's story. Those have been the constants in my own exercise of this office, and they have shaped the curriculum and pedagogy of my forty-four years as a teacher. But what are the possible renovations and additions to this old house?

Dialogue with Culture. Some things are obvious. The dialogue is lopsided; the powerful and invasive culture to which we are all hooked up relentlessly is doing most of the talking. You have only to walk down any street—or even drive your car—to see this: people with eyes and ears tuned in to the constant flow of news, markets, advertising, music, entertainment. Alongside that, we are probably now seeing the third generation of biblical illiteracy.

This illiteracy also reaches to literature. We cannot assume that there is a body of English and American literature that most of the people in our congregations have read. Any appeal to the poets that some of us read—even memorized—in school would be futile. We could go so far as to say that we cannot count on any common cultural experience of weight and significance—literature, cinema, drama, history, biography—upon which to draw.

This has obvious implications for some of my earliest efforts, to connect with culture and interpret the gospel by means of popular novels, plays, and movies. That project holds less promise today, and if it were undertaken would call for a method that does not assume reading or going to the theater. There is, of course, that vast wasteland of television from which occasionally emerge moving stories and images, especially on the public channels. But how many people are tuned into that segment of television and radio?

These days my own sermons subordinate culture to Scripture and tradition. The latest movie or the book I have read, or a cartoon from *The New Yorker*, may provide a hook, raise a question, or show some absurdity in modern life that is an opening for scripture and Christian practice. But if fiction and cinema are to play a significant role in sermons these days, they depend upon being retold—their images and stories presented freshly to the congregation—and the pertinence to Christian proclamation teased out in relation to biblical language, narrative, and images. But it remains true that the juxtaposition—alongside Scripture and tradition—of these secular sources of insight and their probing of the human condition holds homiletical promise. How the elements are weighted, however, is crucial. Despite the afore-mentioned biblical illiteracy, these days we can probably assume that the people in our congregations share more knowledge of the Bible and Christian tradition than of any common corpus of cultural experience. I find myself increasingly using excerpts from prayers and hymns in my sermons; I am somewhat surprised by that.

Preaching as Self-Expression. Most likely, we are uncomfortable with this proposal, and perhaps that discomfort rises from the preoccupation of the early twenty-first century with self-expression: eccentricity in dress, speech, and self-decoration; indifference to manners; reality TV; and media focused on individual experience. These days, self-expression in the pulpit might seem to be too much tuned in to popular culture.

Some people in the room—the five "Venerables" for sure—learned to apologize for bringing personal experience into the pulpit. "If you will pardon a personal reference," was the formula. Self-revelation in the pulpit—relating personal stories, or displaying one's own feelings—was a distraction from the business at hand.

During my own training, a favorite text for warning students away from being too personal was 2 Corinthians 4: "We preach not ourselves . . ." By the time I began to teach preaching, we were questioning this prohibition, and for good reason. Suppressing personal reference, it seemed to some of us, could cut the preacher off from the affective sources of both exegesis and proclamation. Robert Raines, former director of Kirkridge Retreat and Study Center, once put it to me this way: "The Bible is just so much wind until you put up your life as a sail."

But we may want to revisit this matter. For one thing, personal expression these days appears to arouse more curiosity than interest, to use Erich Fromm's distinction. Talk shows and even the newscasts reveal much more about individuals—including notable public figures—but these biographical revelations are in most cases for entertainment, not edification. The format of these shows mirrors the checkout-counter tabloids and reduces the human condition to curiosities. In many cases, we see the commercialization and trivializing of human experience.

Also, a congregation can be completely distracted by curiosity about the preacher who, sometimes inadvertently, reveals something personal. At a parish where the people did not yet know me well, I mentioned in a Sunday sermon a conversation that morning "while shaving." Later, the rector asked me, "Do you realize that some people in the congregation spent the rest of the morning wondering who it was with you in the bathroom this morning?"

Most likely, if Phillips Brooks were giving the Beecher Lectures today, he would define preaching in much the same way as he did in 1877, but with one change: "Preaching is the communication of Truth through *personhood*" (rather than "personality"). Christian faith at its core has a great stake in biography, the telling of the human story. The moment of preaching—what Sittler called "the preacher's whole existence concentrated at the point of declaration and interpretation"—inevitably involves self-expression. What comes to expression in that moment can be so all-consuming and preoccupying that it wakes a man or woman in the middle of the night, stirs the heart or provokes the mind in the middle of a play or a television show, or makes us run with a book open to the page to write down what has just struck us as gospel truth. We cannot begin to preach without that, can we?

The sermon—is it too much to say?—is the Word becoming flesh, through the oh-so-human medium of a person who reads, listens, feels, struggles, laughs, and cries. One's unique personhood must find its way into exegesis, and into the composition and delivery of sermons. It is what Sittler called the "anguish of preaching." It was what Steimle meant when he told us one day that we must preach "from the soles of our feet." It is what you can see in someone like Seiji Ozawa conducting the Boston Symphony: the music is the thing, but what happens there between Beethoven and the orchestra, and through it to the rapt audience, is a matter of his understanding, feeling the music, and putting *himself* into it.[5]

There is a scene in the movie *Three Weddings and a Funeral* in which, as the bride comes down the aisle, the novice priest is fixing his vestments, almost primping. He never gets past that preoccupation with himself, to enter into the human moment, to bring the true gifts of his heart and mind to the celebration. That would not be what we mean by self-expression in the pulpit. It is a matter of being present, as a believable man or woman. We do have this treasure in earthen vessels (again, 2 Corinthians). But these days it would be easy for a preacher to sell that idea short.

Telling the Story. Storytelling is risky business. Story is easily confused with anecdote. Storytelling can be reduced to mere entertainment. A good story can take over. That is, of course, what we expect from a good story, that it will take us over. But the compelling story can obscure or displace the stories of the Bible that are trying to shine through. The snappy illustration can become a substitute for the real stories, the ones most needed— however many times we have told them, however worn they seem—the ones we really need to hear. It is small wonder our homiletics professors warned us about stories.

But Jesus the preacher tips us off to the need for storytelling and shows us how to do it. The story that rings true to human life, that aims to reveal the ways of God, and that trusts the human imagination as a way to truth is needed as much as ever. In fact, many of the church's woes and much schism could be attributed to a failure of imagination—in our moral struggles, in biblical interpretation and theological inquiry, and in our weekly sermons. We need more, not less, of the irony, playfulness, and teasing metaphor of Jesus' parables.

These days the stories that find their way into my sermons are likely to come from three sources: the accumulating experience of a long life—as Frederick Buechner puts it, "life piles up"; pastoral situations, among which baptisms, weddings, and funerals are very rich sources; and the accounts on public radio—occasionally on television and in *The New Yorker*—of real people, their mundane, heroic, and comic lives. What all of these have in common is that they are recognizable as believable human events, in language that we can own. As commonplace as Jesus' parables and often as provincial as our hometown, it is in such stories that the extraordinary is present in the ordinary. Writing about poetry, W. H. Auden described also the possibility of preaching:

> A poet's hope, to be like some valley cheese,
> local, but prized elsewhere.[6]

I want also to tell the church's stories: from the Bible, the saints—ancient and modern—the stories behind our hymnody and prayers, and those that unfold with the church year and in the long procession of faith. Occasionally there will be a movie or a novel, a poem or a scene from a play, that grabs imagination or stirs the heart. When that happens there is a good chance of a connection—by way of moving the preacher—to lection or liturgy. Then, light shines in both directions, the divine-human word in homiletical form. When that happens we know that storytelling is worth the risk. More cautious about the possibilities of the popular arts as sources for preaching, I want nonetheless to continue to tell all sorts of stories that can serve The Story.

The Freedom of the Liturgy. Standing close to baptistery and table the preacher finds a place of freedom: freedom from didacticism and from the need to be exhaustive; freedom from the pressure of mere performance; and freedom as pastor and prophet. In the liturgical action of Holy Baptism and Eucharist, the story comes through with profound clarity and beauty. The need to explain, to moralize, and to grow dogmatic flies out the window. The preacher, while always called to careful exegesis and disciplined, imaginative use of language, need not stand in a spotlight or carry the entire weight of worship. The whole of the liturgy carries the Word. This liturgy at its best is porous, not monolithic, giving the congregation opportunity for silence and diversity of interpretation and application, a rich context for the spoken word. This porous liturgy is the work of the whole people of God, and it gives the people room to do their imaginative and prayerful work. And, in the context of Christ's gracious invitation, the prophetic voice can be heard. The prophetic call is to be the people we already are, baptized into Christ's body and guests at his table. Here, preaching can be a true event of the gospel, as H. H. Farmer has said, at the same time "ultimate demand and final succour."[7]

At the baptistery and holy table we come into what Steimle called a *spacious* place, the place we call salvation, a gracious and open place. Here, gathered with a community close to the water and ready to receive the bread and wine, the preacher is set free by the palpable gospel to find the words and to meet the people without fear, in the abandon of people remembering who they are and sitting down to eat together, ready to speak to each other the truth in love.

During my three years in seminary in Kentucky I served a small congregation up in the bluegrass country. When they learned I was coming to Lexington for the Re(New)ed Homiletic conference, they asked me to come to a supper at the church. I had wondered what it would be like to go back there. I have changed denominations since I was their pastor and taken a journey that might well distance me from those rural Baptists with whom I once lived and served so easily. But they, of course, had the easy solution to our seeing each other after so many years: we would just sit down and eat together. And so we did, telling stories freely and turning into laughter embarrassing and even painful moments that time had healed. I was able, at last, to tell them that I was the one who on my second Sunday as their pastor loaded up all the fake flowers in the church and dropped them off of the Gratz Bridge into the Kentucky River! We had a good time, gave thanks, and parted more aware of the grace of God that keeps us and holds us together. Around the table, remembering, we found a spacious, gracious place.

This spacious situation accommodates a postmodern view, a place to question the merely objective, neutral, and universal: settled, static theology; moral pronouncements divorced from personal reality; absolute certainty about anything really important. Instead, we can embrace our historical life and contemporary reality with frank self-awareness, irony, and even playfulness. Do we not, after all, see that in Jesus, who is so completely available in the moment, there for the actual person standing before him?

Remembering our baptism, and together holding out our hands to receive Christ's gifts, we find the freedom to be human together and to speak the truth in love.

It is this that we can hope for in preaching, those of us who intend to engage our congregations where they live: giving ourselves without fear to this vocation; sinning bravely in self-revelation; and telling the stories old and new as if our lives depended upon them. When that happens, there is no moment in human experience more alive than the Word made flesh in a preacher.

Responses

Mary Alice Mulligan

Each of our twentieth-century "Venerables" spent considerable energy to resuscitate the pulpit during a season of uproar, when homiletics had been left lifeless on the beach, abandoned as archaic and effete. Of the five, perhaps Charles Rice is least known, yet his narrative homiletic resembles people on the ground level of a human pyramid, whose quiet strength and unfailing stability allow others in the spotlight to perform in safety. Father Rice remains committed to his "dialogical, self-expressive, storytelling homiletic," acknowledging preaching as one moment in the liturgical whole. His approach is clear-cut, but not simplistic, with cultural and religious analyses resulting in contemporary alterations to his theories. Below, I consider three of his topics more closely.

Social Analysis. Society was changing dramatically as Charles Rice stepped into the field of homiletics. Transformations continue in secular and religious settings. The divide between wealthy and impoverished widens. Technology makes the incredible possible. Personal freedoms abound at the same time our addiction to various screens eviscerates our imagination. Some years ago while teaching a college philosophy class, I attempted to find a single book everyone had read. Some students had not read *Beowulf*, *Julius Caesar*, *The Scarlet Letter*, *The Invisible Man*, *Catch-22*, *Beloved*, or any other suggested work. The closest we got was *Tom Sawyer*, which five students had not read but had seen one or another movie adaptation. Rice correctly notes, we do not have a shared secular culture today (whether we ever did is a question for another article). He pointedly expands this into the religious realm, describing the spread of "free-floating religiosity." Without shared texts, culture, or experiences, our rampant individualism encourages people to choose from a smorgasbord of religious morsels. I believe the situation is worsening. Bowling alone is sad enough; believing one can figure out cosmic truth alone is horrendous. Sociologists track the opposition to institutional religion. In 1978, Gallup found 81 percent of respondents believed a religious group is unnecessary for arriving at religious beliefs. Wade Clark Roof and William McKinney call it "do-it-yourself religiosity." The believer is her own religious authority.[8]

We need to investigate further the lack of shared cultural experiences coupled with a majority attitude that individualism is appropriate, that whatever works for me is acceptable, that getting ahead matters most. How do we get these shared traits if not from shared cultural experiences? What *is* shaping our culture and how are those forces leaking into the church? Preachers must not ignore either the secular or the religious forces shaping who people are. This leads us right into the next piece.

Role of Dialogue. Religious leadership has always had to strike a balance between liturgical Gnosticism (using language and metaphors only the seriously initiated can comprehend) and secular dilution (where cultural images and language overwhelm the theological freight). The necessity of homiletic dialogue with culture is one of Rice's most helpful ingredients for assisting the preachers' task. Early on he attempted "to interpret the gospel by means of popular novels, plays, and movies." Curiously, after admitting secular culture "is doing most of the talking" in the dialogue, he acknowledges shifting to retelling biblical stories, hymns, and prayers of the church in his preaching, because of the lack of shared secular material.

This is important, but preachers must also push deeper into the function of dialogue. I assert the goal is not to interpret the gospel using cultural tools but, rather, to shine the light of the gospel on culture. A story from seminary illustrates. When the student asks the professor, "Will my sermon do?" the professor naturally replies, "Will it do what?" My question to Rice follows: In the dialogue between culture and pulpit, what is the conversation to do? Since people are biblically illiterate (into the third generation) and experience no shared literature, art, or drama, preachers have the perfect opportunity to assist shaping not only the identity of the gathered congregation, but of the scattered church that moves beyond the sanctuary walls six other days a week. The "dialogue" must be evaluative. When culture advocates individualism in matters of ethics, morals, life choices, religious beliefs, social relations, and interactions with the world, preachers must be prepared not only to engage those ideas, but to refute them theologically.

People *have* shared cultural experiences, even if they have not seen the same movie or read poetry for years. They know children are abandoned, estranged husbands brandish guns, and reality television encourages cut-throat tactics and sensationalism. Even if our congregants have not read *King Lear*, part of it can be used to unify a congregation's sense of offense when unfaithful daughters seem most loved. Then, the sermon can theologically interpret such pain and injustice. Responsible dialogue does more than exchange ideas; it must offer a theologically solid response to the forces at work in society that are contrary to the purposes of God. Of course, those places where God's purposes are championed outside the church must also be recognized, noting how the Spirit is active in the world. Sermons must offer an ethical footing for people who live in society. Dialogue is crucial, but it must interpret society and help shape a theologically sound identity for the congregation.

The Word Made Flesh. At least as early as 1979, Rice was concerned for the Word to become flesh in preaching.[9] Real preacher flesh works in tandem with the flesh displayed in biblical narratives. The reality of human flesh is best comprehended through the use of story. For decades, Charles Rice's assistance in stressing the essential usefulness of story has been unparalleled. However, using *personal* story has always seemed counterproductive to me. For just as society touts individualism and reliance on personal whims to decide theological questions, the preacher's use of personal story reinforces these tendencies. Susan Bond clarifies: "Preachers who make frequent use of personal illustrations imply that personal experience is a valid norm by which to adjudicate theological claims."[10]

Although not directly articulating this, Rice offers an important corrective along these lines, by adapting Phillips Brooks's famous dictum that preaching brings "truth through personality."[11] Rice asserts, "Truth through personhood." The aim is not for listeners to comprehend the individual personality of the preacher but, rather, our common personhood communicated through the sermon. Preachers share flesh with the congregation, and thus share the same joys and struggles (a shared human condition).

But there is an essential piece that Rice's apparent low doctrine of the Word underplays. Namely, we need to see where the *Divine* Word becomes flesh. Congregants are desperate for a glimpse of the Divine Word enfleshed. John tells us *God* the Word became flesh and lived among us. We yearn to perceive *that* flesh. Church people eagerly report they want to know more about God from sermons.[12] Where is the Word of God among *us?* The sermon needs to assist engaging us in life with God. It must show where God has become enfleshed in the Sunday school class who pays to put a shower in the church building for homeless neighbors to use, and in the family who decides to open their home to foster children, and in teens who organize to deter bullying in their school. Divine flesh is at work among us, in our own flesh.

A quick review of Charles Rice's publications reveals a continuing effort to refine his ideas in light of new circumstances. I welcome this opportunity to dialogue with him.

Cláudio Carvalhaes

Charles L. Rice has produced a very important body of work that we all need to visit and revisit from time to time. Any re(new)ed homiletic for the future needs to ponder and consider his insights and proposals. One of the most important contributions he has offered us is drawing a correlation between the preacher and the whole of the liturgy. Especially important is his balancing of the liturgy and the place/importance of the preacher when he says, "The preacher, while always called to careful exegesis and disciplined, imaginative used of language, need not stand in a spotlight or carry the entire weight of worship." The liturgy as a "porous place," as he puts it, is indeed the work of the whole people and not a building up of a moment for the preacher to show up; the liturgy is indeed the whole story told and not a preparation for the consummation of the preacher and his own story. The other contribution Rice gives us is the emphasis on the telling and retelling of the story. "Storytelling is a risky business," he says. Later, he speaks of ". . . telling the stories old and new as if our lives depended upon them." The Bible stories woven in our stories, the stories of the world and vice versa, are what hold us together, what make us live, what shape our lives and give contours to the world. Our task as preachers is to weave those life stories together as if we depended upon them.

Rice's essay provides us a wonderful reading of the changes in North American society during the last forty years. As a note of caution, it is good to remind the readers that when he talks about the *American culture*, he is not talking about the American culture in Chile, or the American culture in Mexico, or the American culture in Honduras. He is talking about part of the North American culture in the United States. Throughout the paper there is a feeling of melancholy about the changes and the loss of what he saw, lived, and knew when he first started his Christian journey. The field of theology still had high importance in the cultural life of this country; people would still pack the churches on Sunday morning; the Word was the medium of the Christian message; and the preacher was still a revered figure in society. Forty years later, we definitely live in another world. Random information has become the new guiding principle in society, people no longer go as often to church on Sunday mornings; iPhones, iPods, YouTube, Facebook, and virtual relationships have replaced the dominance of the spoken word; and the continuous replacement of celebrities are now the temporary revered icons that draw our attention. Rice is very aware of those changes and how they have affected all of us.

However, it seems that he does not know what to do with these changes since he does not offer new ways of dealing with preaching in the midst of these changes. As a matter of fact, when he talks about renovation, he says, "I find myself surprisingly close to where I started," hoping that the story will come alive again and again. The way he goes about preaching is by weighting the elements of tradition and Scripture. One way he finds to recover that juxtaposition is by "increasingly using excerpts from prayers and hymns." Again, his nostalgia for a richer tradition, for when people knew a little more about literature and the Bible, is the place where he leaves us. The gospel of the 1960s and '70s seems to be more sound than the one we preach today. Near the end of the article, he hopes that we will discover again and again the story of Jesus in a way much like the woman with whom he shares orchestra seats holds a thrilling romance with the seats of the Verizon Hall. "Oh, isn't it wonderful? Just look at these seats!" she says, marveling again and again about the seats she visits on every musical presentation. Her reaction to "these seats" surprises her husband who says, "You sit here every year." This state of awe is what Rice hopes for; I suppose that is what we, all of us preachers, are hoping for, is it not?

I suppose I do hope for it, too. However, the thrilling romance with "these seats" will not come just by showing up on Sunday morning. At some point we might not even see these seats there anymore because the whole dynamics of society have changed. People are neither going to church nor listening to classical music the way they used to, and this nostalgia will take us nowhere. We need a shift, a shift that will welcome the new without losing the old. Thus, the same way that the "baby boomers are beginning to pass their wealth on to their progeny, some thirty trillion dollars . . . ," they will also need to pass on the wisdom they gained and the ways of the gospel they knew and practiced. Moreover, they will need to figure out how to live and engage with the new shapes, forms, presence, and possibilities of the story of Jesus in our days.

Rice mentions the resources for his sermons: experiences of life, pastoral situations, accounts from public radio, occasional television shows, and articles from *The New Yorker*. What they have in common, he wisely says, is that they are "recognizable as believable human events in a language that we can own." Two comments:

1. *Life experiences.* If we are to make this story come alive again and again, we will need to broaden the sources of our resources. The world has changed and the United States is not what it was forty years ago. Also, those sources will not bring us all that we need to know in order to preach the gospel faithfully. Thus, the dialogue with culture that Rice proposes must take on a whole new array of issues and themes and life experiences with people other than the ones with whom we are used to living. On one hand, the Internet, rap music, virtual realities, virtual identities, Web relationships, games, iPods, and iPhones make our world a very different world from the one in which Rice grew up. Notwithstanding, the United States will soon have no large majority ethnic groups anymore.

Thus, rubbing shoulders in church and in our daily lives with blacks, immigrants, foreigners, and poor people will definitely give us a different sense of life and pastoral experiences, and these lived experiences must be the resources for our preaching.

2. *Language.* We need continuously to learn a new language because the gospel is fundamentally made up of a language that we do not and cannot own. Caught up in a Babel-tower society, preaching has to do with learning a language that is foreign to us, a language of the Spirit, a language that we cannot "own," and that we learn as we go. This unbeknown language of the gospel is also located in the language of those we do not know and are not familiar with, and that is what makes preaching frightening. We will only know the full story of the gospel as we venture into the stories of those whose languages are foreign to us. There, at the scary and unsafe place of the other's language, is where we might figure out the fullness of God's revelation to us. For this revelation requires our losing our bearings, getting lost on the way, engaging in difficult dialogues, and staying in unpleasant reunions. If we are too attached to our own community and to our own language, our experiences will always be the repetition of the same and our preaching always a preaching to the choir. As a result, classical music would be all that there is. We must stretch ourselves in other directions, to other groups of people, so that we can also preach a story that we do not fully know, with a language that we do not own.

To conclude, the metaphor of "these seats" can run the risk of proposing Christians as voyeurs of the gospel. We are not called to listen to the story of the gospel only but, mostly, to act upon it. If we are to engage new generations of people enjoying "these seats" the same way that this woman does, we are to change the ways we attend to our craft. The story of the gospel will only engage our awe if we become history makers, if we take the Christian task of being co-creators of the world with God, and if we go about figuring out together how to live the "costly grace" of this redemptive story. Thus, the preaching task of the people of God is not only to show up at the church, but to weave the stories of the people of God into the stories of the

Bible, the story of Jesus Christ, and then back to people's daily lives by using various movements, dissonant sounds, strange vocabularies, and practicing different liturgical/citizenship actions of praise, justice, mercy, healing, and transformation.

In any case, Rice does not leave us at loss in his nostalgia. He guides us through this movement by proposing a freedom of liturgy as a porous place and a gracious space: "Around the table, remembering, we found a spacious, gracious place." Yes! I do believe that it is around this gracious place that we redraw the world, that we figure out a space for each other, for each other's stories, for our struggles, and for the continuous, thrilling romance with the story of Jesus Christ.

Inductive Preaching Renewed

Fred B. Craddock

And It Came to Pass

In the fall of 1965, I entered my first seminary class-room as a professor of preaching and New Testa-ment. I was armed with a degree in New Testament from Vanderbilt and a copy of Broadus and Weath-erspoon's *Preparation and Delivery of Sermons*, which had been the textbook for my one preaching class in 1952.[1] I was aware in 1965 of the revolution of the '60's—a social revolution, a sexual revolution, a drug revolution—and the establishment of Berkeley, California, as the new capital of the New America. What I was not aware of was how deeply the revo-lution had made an attack on tradition and author-ity, which included the pulpit. Among my students, I heard a lot of things, none of them complimentary. It was only my first semester, my first attempt to teach preaching, and one of the first things said at the beginning of the course was, "Professor, I guess you know that preaching is for dorks, for the ones who can't do anything better." Students were anticipating ministries, but ministries that had no pulpits. Protests, social action, civil change—those were the orders of the day and that's the world into which I moved with my copy of Broadus and Witherspoon.

The students were in favor of changing the course in preaching from a requirement to an elective. Seminaries across the country dropped preaching entirely from the catalog. Once in a while a school would, under pressure from a few of the dorks, have a retired pastor from the community come out on Friday afternoon and share a few toothless reminiscences of his ministry. And that was homiletics. I went to faculty meetings and heard motions concerning the field in which I was called to teach. A motion was made in faculty that we drop homiletics as a requirement. A motion was made in faculty that we remove the pulpit and the pews from the chapel and sit around on the floor in small groups and reflect on something. A motion was made in faculty that we replace preaching with a course in multimedia communications.

Now, Walter Ong was writing on a more academic level, was writing about what he regarded as the change of the human sensorium, a change in the human antenna. He argued that we pick up signals now not through the ear but through the eye, and the real action is occurring at the eye not at the ear. There were dissertations written on the shorter attention span, and I read a very interesting dissertation on the sound bite as the sermon of the future. The model for communications in those days was a television program called *Laugh-In*—little bits of humor, little bursts of humor, but no continuity, just short-attention pieces.

There were some efforts to rescue preaching. One of them said, let's all accept the fact that Constantine is dead; there is no emperor to make Christianity the official religion of America. We have to make do on our own and pull our own weight. There is no guarantee, no social, or political, or economic underpinning. And there were casual conversation sermons in which the minister came out, leaned on the corner of the communion table, and said, "What do you all want to talk about today?" And, of course, there were dialogue sermons—one at the pulpit, one at the lectern, talking to each other in front of the congregation. Those were efforts, sincere efforts, to rescue homiletics.

It was in the '60s that we had the Second Vatican Council and a revolution in the thinking of the Roman Catholic Church about preaching. All the Protestants were going one way, and here came the Catholic Church with a reaffirmation of the sermon. Thomas Aquinas said, "The primary duty of the priest is to preach the gospel," and I went with Gene Linehan, a Jesuit priest, around the United States and Europe holding conferences for parish priests to introduce them to preaching. It was a painful thing, I went along as a homelitician, a Protestant observer. It was a moving thing. At one of those meetings Gene came out on the platform—he was barefooted, had on those little whitewashed pants, and a skivvies shirt—and said, "I am fifty-six years old, and all my years as a priest I have worked with my back to the congregation. And now my leader says turn around. I have spoken in Latin and now my leader says turn around and speak in the vernacular of the people." He went on and on and on about the change and said, "As you can see, all my armor has been stripped from me. I have nothing left but God," and asked them to stand and sing "A Mighty Fortress is Our God." It was almost a lynching. Gene Linehan made a great contribution to his church. So did Domenico Grazzo, who taught priests that preaching is not a sacrament but is sacramental in nature.[2] I tried to get my students to read his work, but they were busy painting signs to protest something in town.

I don't want to characterize the time as a completely barren time. There was enough raw material available to rescue homiletics. It was lying around all of us. J. L. Austin developed speech act theory and introduced us to the performative power of words.[3] My, what a friend to the preacher that is. James Conant wrote brilliant essays distinguishing between two modes of thought—inductive and deductive.[4] And there was Amos Wilder. His "The Word as Address, and the Word as Meaning" is a marvelous essay, still valuable to read.[5]

There were some new accents on listener responsibility as well. In participatory theater, you went to a play and didn't just observe what was going on stage. The characters on stage would come out and incorporate you into what was going on, would have you take part in the play. Edward Albee said that anyone who comes to see one of his plays must bear some of the responsibility. This was an interesting shift to listener responsibility.

Similarly, in theology, there was a reaffirmation of the priesthood of believers. And in biblical studies, there was the group, mostly German but some American, dealing with Word of God and church and interestingly enough, locating the Word of God in the ear. The Bible is the Word of God when heard (going back, of course, to Luther, who claimed that preaching the Word of God is the Word of God).

Most helpful for me, I think, at that time were studies of the parables of Jesus, the extraordinary communication method of Jesus. And central to these studies was C. H. Dodd's memorable little definition of parables: "A simile, or metaphor, drawn from nature or common life, leaving the mind sufficient doubt as to its precise meaning so as to tease it into active thought."[6] Ah! That's important for preaching. I made note of it, but I didn't know what to do with it because I was still carrying around my Broadus and Weatherspoon. It's hard to turn it loose when you don't have any other place else to go.

We began to read in biblical theology and biblical interpretation about the polyvalent nature of Scripture. A text can generate not just a single meaning but a variety of meanings. This again put responsibility on the listener/reader of the Scripture. So it was, in those days, that I made a move in my own teaching away from the deductive, away from starting with a conclusion and going down. This mode of logic assumes a certain authority on the part of the speaker and the speaker's resources. Places of authority were toppling and you just couldn't begin with a conclusion and clear your throat and say, "Therefore, point 1, point 2, point 3." Where did you get the conclusion? Well, I moved from deductive preaching to induction in the pulpit, in which you begin with particulars and move toward a general truth. The accent was on the listener. Preachers invite the hearers to arrive at their own conclusion. I found this to be congenial to the scientific method: examine particulars and draw a conclusion, usually a very tentative conclusion. Scientists would not say, "All white rats have pink eyes," if they examined ten million that had pink eyes. They would say, "As far as we have examined, white rats have pink eyes." They would not say they all do because there is one white rat somewhere that does not. The movement is inductive, from the particulars to the general.

In inductive logic, I found a map congenial to the methods of exegesis in which I was trained. Exegesis is inductive. You do not come to the text with a conclusion and make it fit (or at least we are not supposed to). Instead, we examine the particulars of a text and arrive at a conclusion as to its meaning. We visited again Romans 10:17, "Faith comes by hearing." We start with the ear. Preaching is to satisfy that: faith comes by hearing. It is, I said to myself, unfair to arrive at a conclusion in private and then announce the conclusion in public. Why not let the listeners arrive at a conclusion? It isn't fair in the race we call preparation of the sermon for the minister to have a ten-mile head start.

And there was the debate on the issue of point of contact. "Point of contact" refers to the gospel meeting the human ear. Is the ear able to receive it? I was more with Rudolf Bultmann than with Karl Barth. I believe the Bible starts with Genesis 1, not Genesis 3. I know, I know, I believe in sin. I have several friends who have sinned. But I also think if you stir around in the wreckage of Genesis 3, you will find a lot of fragments of Genesis 1. So I stood with Bultmann, who said that in every one of us there is a faint recollection of the garden of Eden. To preach inductively, I have to assume the capacity of the listener to take some responsibility in hearing. The accent I made to myself was on evocative vocabulary. It would draw out of the listener's thinking, feeling, and new words.

I felt that we should accent movement rather than structure. I was taught structure. All my sermons looked alike. You could have brought in a photographer and every week they would have looked exactly alike. But nobody was taking pictures of my sermons. You hear a sermon. A sermon is vibration of air across the eardrum. So movement comes before structure.

So it was that I prepared seven essays on preaching in the inductive mode. I took them over to the science building on the campus of Phillips University in Enid, Oklahoma. They had a printing press over there for printing materials for teachers to use in class. I asked if they would print those seven essays, and I gave them the title *As One without Authority*. They said they would print them, but I would have to pay for the project because there was nothing in the budget for it. So I had them print two hundred copies. They were not put together well, there was not enough glue in the spine, and the pages all fell out. Somehow a copy got to Yale, and the dean wrote to me and asked if I would send him another copy because his was all over the floor. Well, so was mine. I prepared the seven essays to use in class, to walk through them with my students with never any expectation or notion that anyone beyond the campus would read them. And that's how it started.

However

From the beginning, however, I have been somewhat haunted by what I did. Was there in what I suggested an abdication of authority in ministry by relocating the authority in the ear of the listener more than at the mouth of the speaker? Is there a cowardly profit in the method? "You won't just come out and say it, Fred. You've got to do this inductive, indirect stuff."

Was there excessive accommodation to the times? The times were all about change. Was I just going with the flow, honoring the culture more than I was honoring the tradition of preaching or the importance of preaching? Did I fail to remember that preaching is not cultural but countercultural? I run into that all the time now that I work with the poor in southern Appalachia, appeal to people for resources to do the work, and mention the condition of the poor—thirteen million children in this country go to bed hungry every night—and they say, "We didn't know that." The American people have more exposure to and knowledge of Britney Spears's navel than they do the thirteen million who do not have anything to eat. So was I bending too much to culture by letting it tell me what and how?

Did I expect too much of the listener? Was it unrealistic to expect the listener to come to the sermon with theological and biblical knowledge so that I could make illusions and echoes and indirections and lure them into a new way of thinking? Did I expect them to have more content than they really did? Did I let Søren Kierkegaard seduce me? He said there is no lack of information in a Christian land. Is that true? I worried about that. Are the people to whom I speak willing to accept responsibility for the message? Maybe they are not. "What did you mean by that? You can't be like Jesus telling a parable, we want you to explain it to us." Is that fair? Is that unfair? Was I expecting too much?

Was I really engaged in a game, hitting the ball in the net? Should I have done what I had been taught to do—hit the ball over the net and run around and hit it back and call it a sermon? Did I expect too much? Would my students? Would they use the method I had developed as an excuse to abandon one of the major functions of preaching, to pass along the tradition? Am I giving them a textbook reason for not doing that anymore?

I answered these questions by telling myself, "But we have now a different audience, a different group of people sitting before the pulpit." But it has always been that way. In our time we are witnessing the death of the traditionalists, who were born in the 1920s. They are dying off by the thousands, about all gone. Only a few of them show up on Sunday. The baby boomers, those who were born in the 1940s with their idealism and their hopes for a new world, a new social order, they're retiring now. The new world has not happened. Generation X, born in the 1960s, are cynical about the idealism that was not realized. They have drawn back and centered upon themselves and self-satisfaction. And now the Millennialists, who were born in the 1980s. Those who work in such matters tell me that they are beginning to sound like the traditionalists. The twenty-year-olds want to know what Grandma and Grandpa believed.

And then there's the word *postmodern*. Now we've reached the postmodern—every book on postmodernism you read has a different definition of it, so I will give you the real one and you can throw your books away. "Postmodern" means that science is chastened and humbled by its repeated defeats. Modernism was marked by a confidence in progress: science is going to bring an end to the ills of the world. But science will now say to you, "We're being whipped every day—Parkinson's, AIDS, cancer, Alzheimer's. We're losing, we're losing." The triumphalism of science is not there anymore, there's humility in its place. And the physicist at Princeton with whom I talked about this said, "It's about time some of you preachers become humbled as we have because you are not doing so well yourself." I told him he was out of bounds.

What is postmodernism? It means this is a time when thinkers do not move from mystery to discovery but from discovery to mystery. Not some of us, but all of us, live in a multicultural, multireligious world and we have to deal with the other. I notice in articles now that the word *Other* is spelled with a capital O to represent someone different from myself, someone who used to be halfway around the world that missionaries came back with pictures of but who now lives next door. We've even turned "other" into a verb with the word *othering*. I had not heard the word until I was coming back from California on the plane and sat next to a woman who said, "Going to Atlanta?" I said, "Yes, Ma'am. You?" She said she was. She said, "What were you doing in California?" and I said, "I was at Loma Linda at the school and the hospital and the church. For three days I was with the Seventh Day Adventists." She asked, "Are you Seventh Day Adventist?" I said, "No, I'm Disciples of Christ." And she said, "Never heard of it. What were you doing with them?" I said, "Well, we were working together on sermons, and on church, etc., things like that." And she said, "In other words, you are not Seventh Day Adventist, but you spent time with them." I said, "Yes." And she said, "Then you were othering." I said, "I was?" She said, "Yes, you were." I said, "I'm sorry, I'm not familiar with the term." She said, "My preacher uses it all the time. He's just making us sick with it. Go out and be with others. We ought to get acquainted with others. We ought to relate to others. Others, others, just always othering. If I hear one more time, one more sermon on othering, I think I will just throw up." She said, "Now just look here," and she had the Delta Airlines *Sky* magazine open on her lap. "See this article here, it's written in English, in Spanish, and in Japanese. A few years ago it would have been just in English. But now they've got to other: have it in Spanish, and also in Japanese. It's just a fad. It'll be something else next week. If I just hold out, othering will be gone." I said, "Oh no, it's not just a fad." She said, "Well, I never heard of it before." And I said, "But it was there when Jesus died on the cross, all up the side there, 'Jesus of Nazareth, King of the Jews' in Hebrew, Latin, and Greek—three languages." She didn't say anything else. I didn't want to pull my Bible card, but she was beginning to get on my nerves.

What is postmodern? Postmodern is the belief that experience triumphs over tradition. *My* experience. My experience triumphs over tradition. Postmodernism means that life is full of disconnects, full of uncertainties, and all is relative. What is postmodern? Technology outruns wisdom. We are serving the machinery instead of it serving us. What is postmodern? Primarily, I would say that postmodernism means that there is no metanarrative. That is probably the singular, most frequent use in defining the nature of postmodernism. There is no metanarrative—no narrative beyond the individual stories, just the individual stories. There is no beginning to end, no Alpha and Omega, no purpose and meaning in the universe. It's just not there. You just have to live with accidents and coincidences, trying to connect what few dots you can. But do not try to make a lot of sense out of it. So that is where we are.

Therefore

Therefore, neither my method nor anyone else's method should go without self-critical reflection to learn continually what to abandon, what to modify, and what to maintain. The preacher today or the one in the 1960s must make decisions relative to the character of the culture and we must ask ourselves, "Do I put too high a price on fitting into the culture? Do I have too much of an appetite for that? Do I put a careful check on what I am doing so that the modes of discourse, as well as the content of discourse, are congenial to the nature of the gospel?"

I have been reflecting on the similarities between the culture of the 1960s and the culture of 2007. Maybe my memory is fading, but they do not seem all that different. First, there is the accent on the visual. You know, the screen has come down now. Back then it was some Christian education director with a reel machine rolling pictures down in the church basement, the tape breaks and all that. Now the screen comes down automatically and the words to the praise chorus appear up there. I say words, but it is usually just one word repeated. But, in 1961, Ong talked about the changing of the human sensorium, so that reality is grasped not at the ear by hearing, not by words, but by pictures. Television will totally replace the radio we were told, and multimedia will replace the sermon we were told. And I was just thinking about the noises being made now and it sounds very much the same. Maybe what goes around, comes around.

In reflecting on these similarities, I guess I would have to say that corrections in my method of preaching are not called for so much because the times have changed. Instead, they are corrections that probably should have been made from the beginning. They're not so much culture related as they are related to the congeniality with the human need and with the nature of the gospel. Flaws that may now appear should have appeared back then, but I was too busy trying to rescue preaching and have a job that I did not see it. Some corrections should be made.

The title is misleading: *As One without Authority*. Søren said that. Søren Kierkegaard said, "I speak as one without authority," and it made sense to me. But it was not the right title for the book. It created a lot of anger. A book came out shortly after that, entitled *Preaching As One With Authority*. I never read it. I hate to be chastened in public, so I read other things instead.

Whenever you accent one feature of preaching, you're guilty of not paying attention to others. And if you are one of these people that everything has to come out even, has to be smooth and round, if you want to give equal attention to everything, nobody will pay any attention to you. You have to underscore something. Have you ever used that yellow marker while reading a book, and when you get to the bottom of the page you realize you've underlined every line? Didn't help much, did it? If you underline, you have to underline certain things and neglect others— things that are important and true. But you cannot say it all. That is why every sermon is a heresy. There are a lot of important, good things you did not say, but you cannot say it all. A man and his dog, on average, have three legs. Having said that, the attention I tried to give to the *how* of preaching caused me to neglect, maybe more than I was justifiable in neglecting, the content. I could have given more attention to the content of preaching, and I don't think it would have prostituted the point I was trying to make with reference to the priesthood of all believers and the right of everyone to do her or his own thinking and believing just as surely as you have to do your own dying. I wanted to release the people to be free to do that. But some corrections need to be made.

There is the lack of biblical knowledge among the listeners. I don't think it calls for dumbing down the sermon. I go to a church now and then in which the minister says nothing, is more or less an emcee of the program of different things but does not really preach. I asked, "Why do you do that?" The minister answered, "Well, these people who are coming are just inquirers." I said, "Well, what are they asking and are you answering that question?" And the minister said, "Well, I hadn't thought about that." The lack of biblical knowledge among the listeners does not call for me to dumb down the substance but, rather, to share the substance, to share the content. And this may be a little tricky—to share the content of the tradition and the Scripture, plus to share the content as though all of them know it, but also to share it as though none of them know it. That can be done. You can be dealing with Jesus and the woman at the well and tell it as though they all knew it and you were just reminding them of it, but you go through the whole story as though none of them knew it: "You remember Jesus stopped. It was around noon. You recall this woman came out there . . ." What am I doing? I'm reminding you of this story, but most of the people out there don't know this story. They do not like to feel stupid, however. So I share it as though I am reminding them of it. And they are learning it. And those who do know it are not insulted. They like to hear it again. Tell it all as though none of them knew, and tell it in such a way as though all of them knew. Larger pieces of material, larger pieces of content, I should have been willing to share. It was not that I was unwilling. I just didn't want to take the edge off what I was trying to accent.

I think another change that would be helpful is to respect more the distance between the text and today. The Bible has its own integrity, for instance. The books of the Bible have their own integrity, and I should not be in such a hurry to collapse the distance between that camel rider in the first century and the Toyota Camry rider of today. But the fact that I am getting up sermons, I am tempted—you know, Sunday comes every week—to be in sort of a hurry to get away from what it *said* to what it *is saying* to this congregation. This is a delightful enterprise and a very necessary enterprise, but I have not often allowed the Bible to just say what it wants to say, whether it fits this sermon and this congregation or not. In other words, I should keep on my desk where I study an atlas that reminds me, "Fred, you've never been there. Here are some good stories about it," and a dictionary, "You don't know this, do you? Look it up, look it up, look it up." I keep those two books right in front of me as reminders that the Scripture has its own world or worlds, and I should not just make raids on that world for a sermon. And, therefore, I would urge—I didn't then, but I would now—that the preacher stay inside the text long enough to feel its formative force as well as its informative force. Scripture informs, but it also forms. It takes patience to stay there long enough for that to happen.

I think I would say today—I didn't then—that we should be patient in enabling a conversation between the text and the listener. You know, that is what I'm doing, negotiating a conversation between this congregation and a passage of Scripture. And it never occurred to me back then that sometimes neither one of them want to talk to the other. I force it. The day after tomorrow is Sunday, "Talk!" Even if I were somewhere in Jude stumbling around trying to get out, there are times when Jude does not have anything to say. I have opened up books of the Bible, like Nahum, and Nahum says, "Fred, I don't have anything to say to you today," but I have not given him that respect. I make him, shake him: "Say something!" Then I speak for the congregation, even though sometimes they do not want to say anything to the Scripture. They are just like the people of Israel who said to Moses, "We're scared to go up there. You go up there, and then you come back and tell us what you saw." They do not always want to talk. I would respect that silence.

I think I would more than ever recognize the positive role of the referential use of words as well as the performative power of words. I accented as appropriate to what I was about without apology, the performative power of words. Words do things. That's what J. L. Austin was all about. Words perform; they change things. But words also have a referential use—just passing along information, referring to places, people, and things. And I was a bit too light on that, I think, because sometimes the most redemptive thing you can do is to give the right information. It is like a cookbook. You do not need a poem with pictures of daisies up in the corner and everything. Just what are the ingredients, how long do you put it in the oven, do you let it cool, or what? Information—very helpful and very clarifying and very redemptive. I minimized it, I think.

In view of the absence of a metanarrative—that is, a sense of continuity, of purpose beyond my own individual life, that there is something else going on in the world—I think I would attend more to the continuities in the tradition and in Scripture. This is what Scripture itself does. It has echoes and illusions and references and sometimes even quotations of what preceded it, what preceded it, what preceded it. And it connects the dots for us. We arrive at a certain place, and there is a sense of meaning in all of that. This story is going somewhere. I think it's possible to preach sermons (with or without the lectionary) in which we just chop off little pieces, sermon-size, slice off about a sermon's worth of the Bible and use that. And you can preach for forty years and notch every tree in the forest and still not have made a path through it. I think I would change that and make connections. For instance, in the lectionary recently, we had the parable of the Good Samaritan (Luke 10:25-37). What did the people who heard Jesus tell that story think? Well, the very last book of their Bible, we call it Second

Chronicles, has a story of a civil war between Israel and Judah, and Israel was winning. Israel won. But Israel wanted to press the case and even harm the people wounded on the ground. But the prophet Oded said, "Leave it alone. Go home. You won." And the writer says the Samaritans came out and bound up the wounds of the wounded, set them on their beasts, and took them to Jericho (2 Chron. 28:1-15). Now Jesus' original audience had that in their background. We do not have such a thing in our background. Preachers have to help the people make connections, especially if they lack a metanarrative.

As part of making such connections, I have recently been urging ministers to prepare and deliver a signature sermon. A signature sermon is a sermon that is uniquely your own. It has as its raw material a tradition, a tradition of the church in which you are a part and to which you minister. And your own personal tradition is mixed into this sermon. If your grandchildren forty years from now were to find a copy of that sermon in a chest, it would answer their questions—who was my grandmother, who was my grandfather, what did they believe, what did they do? This sermon would say it. I would preach that sermon the same Sunday every year to the same people. First Sunday of Advent, the anniversary of the starting of the church, some occasion, and announce it as such. I would be willing to wager that if you did that the attendance would build and build and build so that when you announced that next Sunday you are going to preach your signature sermon, you would have more than you have at Easter. People like some help in what is it that the church has believed and does believe, and why do we do this, and why do we do that, and for us to say it with enough personal force that it carries the authority of your own passion. The sermon need not be autobiographical in its nature, but it does not have to abdicate that either. You can figure the mix. It will be good for you and good for the congregation. I know some churches can nibble on what you preach that day. They can nibble on that and survive a long cold winter of not believing anything. It will really be a very helpful, pastoral thing to do.

Having named some corrections to my early work, let me say that none of these corrections call into question the abiding value of what I tried to do in 1965 and following. I still argue today for the core homiletical values I did back then.

Trusting the listeners to arrive at their own conclusions, to do their own thinking and believing in trusting and deciding.

Resisting the temptation of technology and its more intrusive uses, reducing the gospel to a PowerPoint presentation.

Not losing any confidence in the effective power of words, to walk into a hospital room, stick your head in, and say, "Hello." You will fluff the pillow, turn on the light, and open the blinds. Just that one word, do not forget that.

Continuing to employ concrete and evocative language that includes persons as well as ideas. The Bible is full of people, many of whom are named. We have sermons that are just ideas.

To include conversations: the Bible is a book of continuing conversation. God said, Moses said, Aaron said, Miriam said, Mary said, Jesus said—they are talking all the time. Do not just give reports on it, include the conversation.

I will continue to trust that even in the multicultural context, beneath the surface people are more alike than they are different and will resonate to the truth that both of you share beneath the surface. I used to work so hard at being relevant. I think now more about what is really going on, and I notice Flannery O'Connor can write about southern Protestant illiterate preachers and stir a genuine conversation among Jewish people sitting on the porch in the Adirondacks. What do they have in common? One thing: life. Adults, educated adults, sat in theaters, while upon the screen a strange little creature called E.T.—he was sort of greenish brown and had either two or three fingers. I mean, greenish brown with two or three fingers from another planet, and American adults sat there crying and said to each other, "This is the third time I've come to see this." Now do not tell me people cannot make shifts. Maya Angelou came out of the cotton patch of Arkansas and moved the elite of New York. What do they have in common? Life.

I think in all of this I would say that we must prepare thoroughly to the point of freedom. And the freedom of the pulpit requires two things: to know what I am talking about and to believe it is important. But I will not overlook, nor avoid saying to you, that in all of our trust in the importance and the effectiveness of preaching, every one of us, preacher and listener alike, loves to have some time and experience that is unmediated, some experience of God through, beneath, around, or without my sermon. Now you can talk, you have my permission to talk.

Responses

Gennifer Benjamin Brooks

"We must prepare thoroughly to the point of freedom. And the freedom of the pulpit requires two things: to know what I am talking about and to believe it is important." These words, taken from the last paragraph of Fred Craddock's essay, represent not a summative argument but an important contribution to the homiletical conversation and practice of this twenty-first-century period. Despite his somewhat accurate conclusion that it might have been more than should have been expected of the congregation "to come to the sermon with theological and biblical knowledge" and expect them to make appropriate homiletical and theological conclusions, Craddock's directive regarding inductive preaching was the result of investigation and analysis of the homiletical needs of the time. And it is a privilege to be permitted a bird's-eye view of Craddock's experience and thought processes that led to the advancement of preaching as an essential discipline of the church.

The preacher as one both with and without authority cannot neglect the text in developing the content of the sermon. Accepting that a lack of biblical knowledge is widespread across the spectrum of churchgoers, in order to provide the necessary sermonic substance and to do so in a way that both informs the ignorant and engages the informed requires significant preparation. Since "Scripture informs but it also forms," heretic or not, the preacher, as Craddock rightly says, must be selective in the sharing of the biblical story and does so best by staying with the text and delving sufficiently deep into its contents and history to experience both "its formative force as well as its informative force." However, the nature of preaching as countercultural is not widely recognized among preachers or homileticians, and preaching that accedes to the prevailing culture and the societal situation of the moment has become more or less normative.

Craddock's question—"Do I put a careful check on what I am doing so that the modes of discourse are congenial to the nature of the gospel?"—is important to the continuing homiletical conversation. Before it can be fully engaged, however, or perhaps in tandem with its investigation, one must also address the necessity for congeniality of modes of discourse in the prevailing culture and the context of preaching in order to determine whether they are congenial to the proclamation of the gospel. For example, a current conversation might include questions such as: What does one do with the language of hip-hop and what is its place in preaching? How does one use blogging or tweeting to advance the knowledge of Scripture or the message of a sermon?

Another key point noted by Craddock that remains central to both homiletical conversation and practice is "the accent on the visual." Indeed, the visual media and the methods of access have changed, but contrary to Craddock's observation, I think there is a marked difference. Where previously visual media were peripheral to the verbal engagement of preaching, now society has restructured itself around the visual. Whether worthy of applause or blame, visualization is a facet of postmodernism that cannot be avoided or dismissed, and it requires more attention and imagination in preaching than simply including still pictures or movie clips in the sermon.

This brings the conversation back to the issue of preparation that I consider the greatest contribution of Craddock's reflections. How the preacher prepares is important but *that* the preacher prepares is critical. Because no preacher and no sermon should attempt to say everything contained even in a simple text, the method of preparation for each moment of preaching hinges on the preacher's hermeneutic of preaching preparation. In this regard Craddock's definition of heresy with respect to the content of each sermon might be unhelpful to the conversation. That selectivity in one's approach to a text for the specific moment of preaching could in any way be considered heretical (even if the term is applied loosely) might be a source of encouragement for those who still try to cover it all in one surface reading of a text and say it all in one moment of preaching. Such selectivity might instead provide an opportunity to guide the listeners in arriving at their own conclusions based on the interpretation of the Scripture text.

Returning to the reality of biblical illiteracy, the substance of the sermon must be precise, substantial, and succinct with respect to content, and that takes preparation and presentation which, as Craddock also notes, provides substance and content to both regular congregants and visitors such as searchers. Preparation is necessary in order to engage the multiple groups in the congregation, both with respect to their existing biblical knowledge and the generational differences that make application of the text challenging. Applying text to context and maintaining the integrity of both requires multiple simultaneous conversations. Craddock's suggested change that anchors the preacher in Scripture long enough to engage a dialogical relationship with the text is critical for maintaining the integrity of the biblical text in preaching. Allowing the Bible to speak in its own voice requires preparation time and the preacher is called to "be patient in enabling a conversation between the text and the listener." Time for preparation may also encourage patience in the preacher when the text seems silent. A subject of conversation in the greater homiletical dialogue may need to focus on scriptural silence. I believe, however, that every text speaks at all times, but the language and the content of the speech change depending on the context of the preaching moment.

The preacher's attention to the language of the text and all that preceded its usage in the present context connect to form a metanarrative that speaks to the divine/human covenant, which is the unbroken thread of Scripture. This may subsequently facilitate the hearers' connection and enable them to take their place in the continually developing metanarrative. The Bible facilitates continuing conversation with persons named and unnamed within it and with ideas that are concrete and transformative. Continuous preparation enables the preacher's language to be evocative and imaginative in a way that clarifies and connects the realities of text and context within the sermon.

Craddock's argument for the necessity of core homiletical values is also an important subject for inclusion in the homiletical conversation; however, the idea of a signature sermon that is preached to a congregation annually may be a misunderstanding of present postmodern culture. Change and newness is normative for postmodern society, and although a signature sermon may help to provide grounding for a preacher, even with theological and doctrinal foundations, good preaching necessitates continuous movement and development.

Finally, the cornerstone of inductive preaching, "trusting the listeners to arrive at their own conclusions, to do their own thinking and believing in trusting and deciding" continues to have a meritorious place in the homiletical conversation and practice. However, the discussion requires that attention be paid to the unpreparedness of the listeners to do this, and the necessity of the preacher's preparation to enable both preacher and listeners to attain the greatest value from both the text and the sermon.

Ruthanna B. Hooke

It is impossible to imagine the field of homiletics, or contemporary preaching itself, without the contribution that Fred Craddock has made to this discipline and practice. His works, most notably *As One without Authority*, set in motion a major rethinking of the task of preaching—both how to go about it, and the principles that ought to guide it. Almost forty years after the publication of that volume, several aspects of his proposal stand out as having permanently transformed both the theory and practice of preaching. His proposal was field altering in part because it focused attention on two crucial but previously neglected areas of concern: sensitivity to cultural context and attention to form. Craddock was among the first to take the cultural contexts of preaching seriously, and to argue that preaching must adapt to these changing contexts. In particular, he reflected on how preaching must change in response to the radical questioning of traditional modes of authority that was then underway. Even more novel than this sensitivity to cultural context was Craddock's argument about *how* preaching ought to change, since he argued that sermons needed to change in their form as well as in their content. He made the essential but previously much underemphasized point that form and content cannot be disconnected in sermons, and that the form of a sermon has both practical and theological implications. Regarding the question of authority specifically, Craddock noted that the form of a sermon both shapes and is shaped by how the preacher chooses to exercise authority. Hierarchical modes of authority support a monological and authoritarian preaching style. In modernity, when such forms of authority are questioned, these styles of preaching must change to a more inductive, conversational style of preaching, one that moves from particulars of human experience to more general truths, involving the hearers integrally in the sermon event. In *Overhearing the Gospel*, Craddock used Søren Kierkegaard's theory of indirect communication to defend further this democratizing of preaching, arguing that hearing preaching ought to be thought of as "overhearing," so as to give the listeners freedom to claim the biblical text's meaning for themselves.

Craddock offered a well-developed theological defense of his inductive method, pointing out that the way a preacher structures her sermon has much to do with what she believes about how God makes Godself known to us, who we are in relationship to God, and what the church is as that body that is defined by hearing God's Word. Inductive preaching rests on the claim that the Word of God is found not only in Scripture, but that hearers possess the Word also, and therefore they must have authority to interpret the Word. Craddock noted that this claim rests on the anthropological claim that the listener is not totally devoid of Godwardness. Thus, Craddock essentially proposed a different doctrine of revelation, theological anthropology, and ecclesiology than had been advanced in earlier theologies of preaching, most notably that of Karl Barth, one of Craddock's primary interlocutors and perhaps the greatest influence in doctrines of preaching prior to Craddock.

The continuing influence of Craddock's proposal in twenty-first-century homiletics will be felt partly in the sheer popularity of the inductive method of preaching. This sermon form is probably the dominant form in Protestant mainline churches today, and is likely to remain so. Preachers gravitate to this method because they find credible Craddock's arguments in support of it: that Christians today are not steeped in the Bible and need to be led to it through a process of discovery; that hearers are not disposed to accede to authoritarian presentations of the gospel; and that, despite the postliberal argument that preachers should lead with Scripture, the pastoral reality is that hearers need and want to have their own experience honored, even while it is placed in relationship to the gospel. It ought to be possible to do both, and Craddock's method allows for this.

In addition to the prevalence of the inductive method itself, Craddock's proposal will influence the contemporary homiletical conversation by continuing to draw attention to preaching's relationship to its cultural context, and how this context ought to shape sermon form. In light of these concerns, it is worthwhile to explore how cultural contexts have shifted since Craddock's initial proposal, and how his theory might be adapted to address these changes. Two particular cultural shifts call for a reevaluation of Craddock's proposal. First, since the time of Craddock's initial publications there have been both demographic and philosophical shifts toward the recognition of greater diversity. American culture has become notably more diverse, racially, ethnically, and religiously, since Craddock's early work. In addition, postmodern thought has successfully challenged the notion that humans share any common, universal experience. One of the weaknesses of the New Homiletic in general is this presupposition of universal experience. The danger of this assumption is that such "universal" experience is often the experience of the dominant class—white, heterosexual, middle class, and male. The postmodern critique of this assumption does not mean that preachers cannot appeal to any sense of shared human experience (very likely preaching would be impossible if preachers could not do this), but it does mean that all preachers must be self-critical and self-conscious about their own social location. Preachers need to be careful about asserting truths that are taken to be universal for all people in all places. To exercise care in this area is not to accede to relativism; it is not to say that there is no truth out there, but it is to say that each preacher's vision of truth is necessarily perspectival, and is not the whole truth for all people at all times. This is an important corrective to Craddock's proposal because it is this assumption of universal experience that gives to his proposal a kind of back-door authoritarianism: the inductive preacher still knows where he wants the hearers to end up, which is to share the experience of the text that the preacher has had, the assumption being that this experience will be true for all and can be shared by all. Thus, the inductive preacher does not completely abdicate control of the sermon but, rather, wields that control in a more skillful way than the old-fashioned deductive preacher does. Inductive preaching thereby retains a slight hint of manipulation; it is significant that Craddock's work is entitled *As One without Authority*, suggesting that the preacher only *seems* to be relinquishing authority over the sermon, but does not really do so.

In addition to the deconstruction of the notion of universal experience since Craddock's original proposal, a second shift since the early 1970s has been the abating of antipathy toward all forms of authority, such that hearers today are hungrier for visionary leadership. Craddock worries in his essay that his method abdicates too much authority, and indeed, the current cultural moment calls for more authoritative speech from the pulpit than the inductive method often allows. This is particularly needed if preaching is to recover a public or prophetic voice; a thoroughly democratic sermon cannot easily speak a prophetic word, as that word is almost by definition one that people do not want to hear and may well not arrive at on their own. Likewise, Craddock wonders if he slighted emphasis on Scripture in his original proposal, and it does seem that more authoritative, didactic preaching is required in order to commend the Christian faith to an increasingly biblically illiterate public. It is difficult to hand down the Christian faith in a completely open-ended sermon, since while the Word of God may reside in the people, that Word as witnessed to in Scripture and the tradition of the church can only be understood through teaching and learning. These cultural realities suggest that preachers need to claim forms of authority that can help the Protestant mainline claim a public, prophetic, and more distinctively Christian voice.

The necessity to question notions of universal experience and the need for greater authority in the pulpit seem to point preaching in opposite directions, but in fact these two needs can be compatible. Taken together, these requirements suggest a mode of preaching in which the preacher claims her authority more forthrightly, declaring more clearly what she knows and where she stands than inductive preaching often fosters, while at the same time not offering this position as universal truth. The preacher needs to be bolder in claiming the authority that is rooted in her particular perspective on the gospel, and more modest in acknowledging that this is the truth as seen from her perspective, rather than the truth that is universally true for all. This kind of preaching has similarities to theories of preaching as confession or testimony, as recently proposed by David Lose, Anna Carter Florence, and others. Craddock's proposal regarding the "signature sermon," a yearly sermon in which the preacher declares what he believes and why he believes it, has affinities with this type of preaching, which is at once more authoritative and more truly inclusive of the listener than inductive preaching as originally formulated.

Finally, the richness of Craddock's theological defense of inductive preaching can inspire contemporary homileticians to engage in similarly nuanced theological reflection on preaching. For example, Craddock's work invites a fruitful conversation about the theological implications of the doctrine of revelation that supports his inductive method. One danger of Craddock's formulation is that the Word of God might seem to be dependent on human effort—the skill of the preacher in inductively leading hearers to an experience of the text, and the effort of listeners to complete the sermon. This is a weakness of the New Homiletic in general: its emphasis on rhetoric, narrative, and artistic expression suggests that the revelatory power of the sermon depends on the preacher's skill in crafting an experience for listeners, rather than on God's action. It may be that a confessional or testimonial stance on the part of the preacher has the theological advantage of restoring God's sovereignty in the sermon event, since in these models the preacher is not in charge of orchestrating an experience for the hearers, but is only required to confess what *she* believes. This humbler stance creates space for God to act to make the preaching event the Word of God for the hearers. This stance also makes preaching an explicitly spiritual discipline, one in which the preacher sees her task as opening herself to God and the listeners, rather than leading hearers through a skillfully planned process. Whether this understanding of preaching can address the theological issues raised by Craddock's proposal is a matter for further discussion, but Craddock has set the terms for fruitful conversation along these lines. In this area, as in his attention to cultural contexts, his sensitivity to the implications of form, and his proposal of a method upon which thousands of preachers rely, it is evident that Craddock's work will continue to shape the homiletical conversation powerfully in the twenty-first century, just as it revolutionized the field in the twentieth century.

Celebration Renewed

Henry H. Mitchell

I t is with gratitude that I take part in this historic conversation, the need for which is quite obvious to us all by now, and the fruit of which is bound to be of value to us all.

I propose first to outline what I offered in *Celebration and Experience in Preaching* as released in 1990. It was the core of what I had been learning, teaching, and writing since 1964. There were prior bits of insight spontaneously gathered for at least two decades, but there were no dreams, focused preparatory readings, or academic ambitions. The history text entitled *Black Preaching* (1970) eventually emerged, in a sense, from two papers written for a graduate course in linguistics, both of which were published in *The Christian Century*.

Core Contribution

My Beecher Lectures at Yale in 1974 yielded *The Recovery of Preaching* in 1977. This launched me as a thinker and writer about preaching, black and otherwise. By 1990, I had formulated a second homiletics textbook summing it all up, for whosoever would pay attention, regardless of ethnic background or culture.

I opened *Celebration and Experience in Preaching* with a lengthy psychological justification of the folk-generated homiletic method I had extrapolated from the African American pulpit tradition. Whereas European American homiletics had primarily focused on the cognitive consciousness of the hearer, in this folk-generated method I emphasized intuitive consciousness as the sector of interactive human consciousness where faith and trust are retained. Additionally, I claimed that human emotions operate parallel to the intuitive, in another interacting sector of consciousness. Neither, however, was held to be the *source* of faith and trust. Faith and trust are gifts bestowed by the Holy Spirit. Rather, the intuitive serves to keep and care for the "tapes" of holistic intuitions of trust, and the emotive retains "tapes" of deep feelings about that trust as the gift of God.

This emphasis on the intuitive and emotional did not mean I dismissed the importance of the cognitive, but that I claimed for it a different role. We are, after all, to love God with all our *minds*. Rational consciousness frames holistic, gut-level trust into words that express how deeply we trust, and how we feel about that trust. Reason is employed also to weed out the self-contradictions that sometimes creep into our witness, as well as our inner patterns of thought. Thus, the mind is always at work during the expression of belief. Reason is the servant of faith, and we can never believe without using our minds. This understanding of the relationship of the intuitive, emotional, and cognitive consciousness resulted in a holistic homiletic.

With all three of these interacting sectors of consciousness ruled out as *sources* of faith and trust, the question then arises, *Just what is the source?* The intuitive sector is fed with data and insight collected apart from rational processing, but how and by what? The answer is the all-encompassing category called *human experience*. The intuitive quietly accumulates data and insights from exposures in family, school, work, worship, and the culture as a whole. Intuitive insights are often wiser than rational insights, but intuition may also harbor our most erroneous misjudgments and prejudices. In either case, intuition is vitally important.

Our intuitive tapes of trust are recorded from direct and vicarious *experiential encounters with trust*. Direct *or* vicarious, hearers identify with and/or enter into the experience, and take it for their own. The process is a kind of spiritual contagion, not subject to human control or duplication at will. It is this experiential input of trust that good preaching offers, to be used by the Holy Spirit for the saving, growth, and empowerment of the hearers.

In a word, people are not saved by rational ideas and concrete data, no matter how impressive. The Holy Spirit uses *experiences* to record over tapes of unbelief. Once a sermon designer has formulated what is needed for a rational removal of intellectual objections and questions, the preacher's preeminent task still remains: to generate an *experience* of the Word. This is where the greater effort needs to be extended. How, then, is this effort employed in the designing of meaningful experience within the sermonic event?

Experiential encounters with God and the Word are generated through literary vehicles that use concrete imagery, as a parallel to abstract truth, to make it more understandable. More importantly, by the hearer's identifying into the flow of the sermonic imagery, the sermon helps them to trust God and live by the *behavioral purpose* of the scriptural text. These life-changing formats for focused vicarious experience are called *genres*.

The most widely known and used genre is the *narrative*—the story in all of its forms and customary usages. This genre includes story, epic tale, personal testimony, monologue, dialogue, and drama. Any "eyewitness-quality" recounting of human interaction, which has a protagonist, a plot or conflict, and a resolution, is a narrative, by whatever sublabel.

The genre called *character sketch* is simply a series of mini-narratives, each of which illustrates the behavioral purpose of the sermon's scriptural text. The *group study* does for a group, of whatever type, what a character sketch does for individuals. A congregation, for instance, has characteristics and group responses similar to those of a person.

Another genre is the *metaphor*, naturally grouped with the simile. These genres are the "parables" so widely used by Jesus. These achieve the behavioral purpose by means of identification due to familiarity. The main moves in the sermon consist of increments of truth drawn from characteristics of the metaphor. For example, "salt preserves."

In all of these descriptions, I have presupposed a term that needs to be defined—*behavioral purpose*. This concept came to me as an essential element in all stories and dramas. It is related to what some call the central theme, but while the theme gives intellectual focus to a narrative (or sermon), the main function of the behavioral purpose is to motivate the hearer to act in a manner consistent with the text. Literarily, the central purpose holds the story together and is the basis of the suspense and involvement of the hearer. The story may also enhance knowledge. But the bottom line is *behavioral*. Every preacher needs to choose an appropriate behavioral purpose, as opposed to a cognitive purpose such as facts or truth, as a final goal. However little or much doctrine hearers may understand, the gospel calls them to *trust* and *live* by the Word. "All thy mind" applies fully, whatever the IQ, and so also does the grace by which people are saved.

I have not yet done a survey of my homiletic colleagues to ascertain to what extent they agree or disagree on this behavioral purpose. I do know that the one reference I saw was in a kindly mention, where I was given all possible credit or blame. In other words, the author wasn't fully in agreement quite yet. Therefore, it was with great joy that I read in a book called *Story* where Robert McKee, a top guru of Hollywood film writers, declared that every story *has* to have a central (noncognitive) purpose in control.

Contexts in Contrast

The homiletical approach I have described above began to take root in the mid-1960s and grew over two-and-a-half decades. How has the situation changed for preachers today in the early twenty-first century?

I labor among at least three contexts, since I preach and teach in such a variety of cultural communities: African American, majority American, and academic religious American, or seminary. These ethno-cultural groups have grown somewhat closer together in the last half-century, but there is still a long way to go. The greatest progress toward unity has been made among the various seminary communities. Indeed, much of the lay-level movement to unity, as made thus far, can be attributed to seminary influence, as well as to the wider intellectual climate, in which conversations like this one are sponsored.

It goes without saying that to offer any generalizations about cultures is a risky business. With, as well as without, charitable intent, various opinions are widely debated. Yet the ideal goals of unity can never be reached if sincere differences are swept under the rug. With that understanding, let me scan theological trends I have encountered in the culture of academia.

Not claiming to be at all expertly familiar with the recent flood of volumes on preaching, I would say that I sense a movement from deductive to inductive preaching. I think it has been healthy, so long as it has stopped short of extremes. I feel no sorrow for the demise of the three-abstract-points-and-a-poem sermon. Those who love God with their minds ask a lot of questions and insist that faith make sense. Paul Tillich urged us to think to the very limits of human reason before we take the leap of faith. However, both inductive and deductive sermons assume that the cognitive processes are primary. Whether many African Americans know it or not, our pulpit tradition could be said to be basically experiential in the main body of the sermon. Of course, we utilize both inductive and deductive processes on occasion, for such things as interpreting what was first received in the sermon's vicarious *experience* of faith.

In our culture, the last fifty years have not removed the deductive requirement that the preacher first announce a text from the Bible, as certification that this is not mere personal opinion. Until this announcement, we preachers are just talking. After that, we are expected to offer vivid, gripping tales out of the Scriptures, and oratorical *tours de force*. But the vast majority of us still want to know, first, "Is this from the Bible, or is it something you made up?"

It may not be traditionally "deductive" as such, but I would still be uncomfortable without a text to back me up. An apparent exception might be when the text surfaces at the end of the story (inductive), since an early text announcement could kill the suspense. I cannot, however, recall when I ever took the late-text route because congregations know most of the stories and their endings anyway. As in Africa, the suspense in black preaching is related to the artistry of *how* one brings a familiar tale to life once again.

If the popular worship of many television ministries is any measure, sermon texts are still "in," no matter how theatrical and star studded the rest of the program is. A television program, with all its bells and whistles, *can still* have biblical focus and prove its worth in the popular mind. T. D. Jakes's ministry from The Potter's House in Dallas might be such a ministry.

Another trend among some theologians is called *process theology*. It has what might be called open-ended belief; everything is becoming. It is an effective antidote for literalness and rigidity, as found among some middle and upper classes of the American majority. In a culture perennially subject to insecurity and oppression, however, there is a cry for more certitude than is afforded by process theology's open-endedness. In the "Somehow" sermon theme of preachers like H. Beecher Hicks, the openness may be in God's mysterious methods of deliverance, but the *end* of it all is fixed and certain. The "Comfort ye" by which we survive demands more than a "maybe" or a "perhaps." And the justice we demand is not subject to convenient relativity. The kingdoms of this world will surely fall, and so will our oppressors.

A notable aspect of African American church life today is the megachurch and its huge membership spread. While a spontaneous stratification of memberships by class and culture could be seen as far back as the 1830s in the North, today's huge congregations are more inclusive. Trained clergy no longer shun indigenous culture; they actually celebrate it. The result is a healthy broadening of appeal, in preaching and in worship. This approach needs to be even more accepted and utilized in the planning of preaching, worship, ministries, and outreach of the African American churches. Elitism in any pulpit, of any culture, is a heretical denial of the "Whosoever will" invitation (Rev. 22:17). Culturally speaking, we need to be all things to all, that God might save some (1 Cor. 9:22).

In the academic understanding of preaching and the preparation of sermons, it is my opinion that the last fifty years have not greatly changed the Western culture's commitment to preaching as cognitive enterprise. Sermons seek to convince the mind, even though the New Homiletic has attempted to broaden the focus. In African American culture, and among some other thinkers, the sermon is a meaningful, holistic, and life-changing *experience* of God and the Word. With or without conscious intent, the best-educated preachers in the majority culture seem to prepare an *argument* for the mental processes, rather than a profoundly meaningful experience for the whole person.

The design of a holistic experience of the gospel includes cognitive content and meaning, of course, but the ideas and facts, as such, are only the beginning. Faith, hope, and love are not abstract ideas. They are profound emotions and blessed intuitions. To be sure, there are great ideas about them, and they have to make sense, but faith/trust, hope, and love are given by God through vicarious *experience*, not impressive argument. It is my hope that it will not take all of the next half-century to wean the Western mind of the subtle suspicion of the sectors of human consciousness where faith abides, and where the worship of God is most enriching.

Reshaping for the Future

What does this mean for the relevance of my work, and for the whole wide world of homiletics, in the years ahead?

I have just completed an extensive rewrite of my 1990 textbook, *Celebration and Experience in Preaching*. Needless to say, it already contains evidence of things I have learned about homiletics, changes in approach or strategy, and better ways to state all of it. The most obvious change in approach is the radical change to the book's opening. I have moved the first edition's first chapter, a biblical and psycho-spiritual rationale for preaching as experiential encounter, from chapter 1 to an appendix. I know this is important, but it has been clearly demonstrated that when people seek to learn sermon design, they do not expect such a lengthy lecture/lesson in clinical psychology to begin with. It turns them off.

In the new book, the most important lesson in homiletic form, or sermon outline, has been my own growing understanding of the uses of the genre I have called *expository*. A more careful review of this vehicle of experience has convinced me that it is the most important of the six main categories of genre. This is not based on the stereotypical, verse-by-verse form of expository bibliolatry. Rather, it is the result of simple research. This is the most constantly used of all the genres as vehicles of experience, regardless of theological position, and even though, technically speaking, exposition is not really a genre.

While my first textbook devoted much more attention to forms of the narrative genre, the fact is that few preachers, myself included, are gifted with stories that fill out a whole sermon. The same is true of the use of parables, metaphors, and similes. What happens in the best exposition of an abstract text is that the moves in consciousness (traditional "points") are brought to vivid illustration by use of a brief tale or mini-metaphor. An increment of abstract meaning is drawn from the text, but its ultimate purpose is achieved by means of a vehicle of experience, not an abstract exegetical essay.

This is not to be mistaken as a covert attempt to get preachers to do more biblical sermons, although there might be a need for such. Old-time expository preaching bears little resemblance to the Bible encounters of which I speak. Unlike the running commentaries on whole chapters, this exposition usually involves only one verse, or even a part of a verse. This text contains only one behavioral purpose, which is quite adequate for the goal of a whole sermon. This emphasis on biblical texts is motivated by the desire to revive the preaching in every pulpit, regardless of the preacher's theological position. The demand emanates from all directions.

If I were called to engage in a crusade to resurrect preaching and the teaching of homiletics for the coming days, this would be what I would want to focus on. I only wish that, earlier in my own teaching, I had seen this biblical centrality in preaching as clearly as I do now. As a creature of my culture, I just did it.

The second and most challenging element of change for whatever teaching I have left to do would focus more on students' personal development of self-confidence and creativity. I have always had at least one counseling session on outlines with every student. But from here on out, I would want more to emphasize helping students of all cultures to break out of learned limitations, and design sensitive and creatively authentic experiences of the Word. It occurs to me that I have too lightly assumed a natural ability to see and feel meaningful experiences, and then communicate them to others.

For instance, my own breakthrough in this regard is crystallized in the sermon that served as my concluding Beecher Lecture at Yale in 1974. I preached it again as part of the conference from which this essay is drawn and it is included on the DVD of sermons that comes with this book. I see things in this signature sermon now that I did not see twenty-five years ago, and I would now draw out in students today what was drawn from me then: a sensitivity for the details in settings, and in the feelings of people, which call forth in the hearer a vivid experiential encounter. The text for the sermon is Ezekiel 3:15: "I sat where they sat . . ." The behavioral purpose is to move parents and teens to sit in each others' places and bridge the generation gap with mutual understanding. The genre of the main body of the sermon was a character sketch, with Ezekiel as protagonist, embodying the text and its behavioral purpose.

I am amazed at the details in the original that still, as we say, "grab me." My description of Ezekiel's predicament, based on 3:14, attempts to explain why the prophet went in bitterness, in the heat of his spirit:

> From membership in a respected family of ruling priests, he went to an exile in which his people had very fluctuating rights . . . they were expatriates. They were not slaves, but they surely were not free. . . . They couldn't really speak of themselves as their own, and this was a far cry from being a member of a powerful family of priests.
>
> Ezekiel went from a full-time ministry in the naturally air-conditioned hills of Zion, to what was at best a bivocational ministry among the tillers of a sweltering, watery wasteland . . . along a manmade channel off the Euphrates. He went from presiding in the beautiful temple atmosphere at Jerusalem to the very difficult task of organizing impromptu gatherings down by a river, where dispirited exiles found it hard to sing the songs of Zion in a strange land . . . from a secure base in the center of orthodoxy . . . to trying to hold the attention of an audience who considered themselves transients. . . . Housing Project types who hoped soon to go home; divided between the numbing grief of forced expatriation, and the temptation to seek the strength of the gods of their very comfortable conquerors.

It is no wonder that in the verse before our text, Ezekiel confesses that he "went in bitterness, in the heat of his spirit." But the redeeming fact is that even in this mood, he reports that "the hand of the LORD was strong upon him." So the prophet sat where they sat in spirit for seven days, and the change in his attitude is now significant world history. It is not described in the text, but if you sit where Ezekiel sat and then read his writings, the evident impact is awesome: Ezekiel got over his bitter disappointment and identified with his people. He understood that instead of fussing at them for not going to a church with no building, on a Friday night, which wasn't set aside in the oppressor's culture, they were to be praised for engaging in worship *anywhere, at any time.* He had to rejoice that they wept when they remembered Zion (Ps. 137:1).

The contributions he made after sitting where they sat are a blessing to *all* nations and *all* conditions. One such was the doctrine of individual accountability before God. As Ezekiel put it (18:1-4; paraphrase mine):

> You have heard it said that the fathers have eaten sour grapes, and the children's teeth are on edge. Let's not hear any more of that nonsense. As the soul of the father is mine, so also is the soul of the son, and the soul that does the sinning, that's the one that's going to die.

Thus were untold generations delivered from primitive group guilt for the sin of one.

Again, a timeless tenet of sound doctrine is to be found in the deliverance of the exiles from the notion that God was to be truly worshiped in the Temple at Jerusalem, where were kept the Holy Scrolls of the Ark of the Covenant. They wept by the river because the priests had *taught* one single holy place. Jewish religion worldwide has survived the Diaspora thanks in part to Ezekiel's understanding of the omnipresence of God. And all of us are blessed by it as well.

This sermon goes on to apply this example of sitting in each other's place, to close the generation gap between parents and youth. The sermon ends with the following celebration:[1]

> No group is exempt from the obligation to "sit where they sit," and all groups react positively to people who truly identify with them ...
>
> Many of us will say, of course, "That's too much to ask. You're telling me to sit with *those* guys? Man, that's risky." And so it is. But He who calls us never preached behind the privacy and protection of a high wire fence. In my world, there is an imaginatively projected preface to Jesus' Parable of the Vineyard and the Wicked Tenants. It goes something like this:
>
>> In the halls of heaven, God the Father called a conference one day, to review the progress of communication with the tenants on the planet Earth. A report was given on the patriarchs of early Hebrew history, but it was not good. The

report on the judges was not significantly better. The communications report on the kings was terribly poor. There were reports on both priests and prophets, but none had been adequate to reconcile the people to God.

The Father looked to His left and paused briefly. Before He could ask for a volunteer, a voice came forth from the right. It was the Son of God, declaring, "I'll go and try to reconcile them. I'll use a different method; I'll sit where they sit and be close to them, to show our love.

"If they sit in temptation, I'll sit there too."

—*And the writer of Hebrews said, He was tempted in all things like as we.*

"If they sit in hunger, I'll sit in hunger."

—*And the Gospels record that after His forty days of fasting in the wilderness, he was hungry.*

"If they sit in thirst, I'll sit in thirst."

—*And on the cross, He cried, "I thirst."*

"If they sit under a cloud of misunderstanding, I'll sit there too."

—*And John said Jesus asked wistfully, "Will ye also go away?"*

"If they sit in sorrow and tears, I'll sit in sorrow and tears."

—*And at Bethany, Jesus wept (John 11:35).*

"If they sit in deep depression and feel like Thou hast abandoned them, I'll sit there too."

—*And from the cross He cried, "My God, My God, why?"*

Jesus sat where we sit. Lord, let this mind be in us also. Amen!

My 20/20 hindsight into the day that sermon was written, and my subsequent experiences in the classroom, all suggest to me that in the future we will need a variety of new exercises in sermon design, as well as a series of spiritual disciplines to help move toward comparable freedom of inspired creative imagination.

Responses

Valerie Bridgeman

When Henry Mitchell wrote *The Recovery of Preaching* in 1977, and later *Celebration and Experience in Preaching*, he laid bare a method that demystified the emotional response to and in traditional black preaching. His work became one of a number of launching pads for those seeking to make connections in the performative space of preaching, owning that preaching is not the words on a sheet of paper but, rather, the words that come from the mouth of the preacher in a particular way. According to Mitchell's essay, he emphasized "intuitive consciousness as the sector of interactive human consciousness where faith and trust are retained." He sought, as he notes, not to dismiss cognition as unimportant in the preaching event, but to claim a different role for the intuitive and emotional, a nod to the role of experience in the world of the listener. His work was followed admirably by Frank A. Thomas's *They Like Never to Quit Praisin' God.*[2] I agree with Mitchell that the preacher's primary task is to create an experience of the Word. Looking at narrative, character sketch, and metaphor, Mitchell intends to describe how these genres produce behavioral responses.

The homiletics field owes a deep thanks to Mitchell and to his generation of scholars for ferreting out more fully the challenge of connecting the head and heart in the preaching event. In the classroom, I have termed this task as learning "to preach to matter." I mean this double entendre in the same way philosopher and public theologian Cornel West uses "race matters." That is, the proclaimer must seek to say what she or he says about *things* that matter. Preaching ought to concern itself with grand visions that recreate mundane lives. Congregations ought to hear something that matters to their lives, the core of their being, and the reparation of the world. Whatever the preacher says should assume a larger-than-life quality inspiring a faith that one may *be* differently and/or *do* differently.

Second, by "preach to matter" I mean that preachers must be deeply aware that they speak to matter—that is, to flesh-and-blood, earthbound creatures, whose lives are lodged in history. Such realizations require more than mental assent to facts, but also an ability to convey material empathy, to elicit recognition, as in, "I know *that* person; I have *been* that person; I *am* that person." This material preaching goes further than Mitchell's emotive/intuitive categories by expanding the range of what is possible in language use and in performance. Material preaching portends grittier language and metaphors mined from the mother lode of the mundane and profane. Here I mean the root meaning of "profane," that is, "outside the church," though never outside of where God works. Such metaphoric use still draws on biblical language, but also deliberately reaches beyond religious jargon into popular culture. A premiere example of this kind of use is in what is called "hip-hop preaching." Such language reaches beyond contrived, "let me tell you a story" sermon illustrations. Instead, this holy profanity infuses preachers' metaphors with the parabolic everyday stuff of people's lives, jarring and jockeying for position in the hearts of hearers. These metaphors are poetic.

My work on the poetic sermonic form is in nascent stages still. But this form seems to me to be a next, natural step from Mitchell's work. Like Mitchell, and others, my concern is at the intersection of performance and receptivity. I want to create a sermon that is like a poem twice read, a lingering whiff of perfume; the kind of sermon that will not let the hearer sleep; that troubles by its images, a sermon that causes questions to irrupt. This poetic form is rigorous, probably not best left to "Saturday night specials." It is rigorous in that it refuses to explain allusions or metaphors. The form trusts the power of images and words, like yeast in dough, even if the listener has never put her or his hands in the sticky mass of flour, crises, water, hope. Such sermons rely on absurd notions to break open new possibilities, like Jay-Z for Preach or lambs lying down with wolves. Unlike Mitchell, I do not believe that ambiguity or unanswered questions leave a sermon cold, even in traditionally African American settings. Instead, I believe preachers must help build capacity for the angst that all people know while proclaiming the good news that God is present in human affairs.

Going into the twenty-first century, I believe we may build on Mitchell's proposal in at least two ways by using the idea of profane and poetic preaching. One way is to acknowledge that Mitchell's proposal is not merely a "black homiletic" but, rather, an accurate assessment of the ways in which humans, no matter their cultural contexts, experience preaching. Agreeing to this premise would not, in my mind, negate Mitchell's correct assertion that there are very real cultural differences. This caveat notwithstanding, these differences do not negate the creaturely materiality of all people—the earth-bound, history-encoded world of folk. A second way to build on Mitchell's proposal is to explore the seams of sameness and the divides of differences among diverse populations in order to take familiar texts and make them live in the profane world. This task actually pushes Mitchell's notion that preachers are "just talking" until they have made clear the connection in the text. Sometimes, I believe, the connection with the grime of people's experiences, the radical subjectivity of the listener, is the sacred foundation on which the Word itself finds a footing. It is into human places that God's voice carves a space in which to resound. This space is the poet's place—the place where a well-crafted phrase, a vivid description may leave persons sighing as at the end of a good poem, one demanding to be heard again.

A poetic sermon is crafted as a poem. The preacher lines the sermon out in phrases, seeking the rhythm of a poetic reading. It requires the preacher to read her sermon out loud, to know how the words sound together. Below is an excerpt of such a sermon-poem that I used the First Sunday after Easter. The sermon, titled "Dusting for Fingerprints," was based on John 20:19-31, and was preached as a part of the Styberg Lecture Series at the Styberg Preaching Institute at Garrett Evangelical Theological Seminary. Every phrase gives a natural pausing place, giving congregations time to absorb the words and the images and to find themselves in them. After this sermon, which was also a workshop piece, several congregants approached me and quoted phrases from the sermon as well as told me exactly what the sermon had stirred in them, leaving me with the impression and the hope that I had achieved my goal, which was to design a sermon that would linger like a whiff of perfume in the air, returning to the hearer time and again, like a poem twice read.

> In days filled with fear,
> The last thing we want to be
> Is alone with our thoughts,
> Afraid that what we know about God
> Is an illusion, afraid that all our hopes
> Are made of dust—or worse . . .
> That we only imagined a new beginning
> That phoenix risings are the myths
> We believe them to be

When fear grips our throats
And chokes resurrection from
Our minds, we look for signs
That the courage we had—just a week ago
Was based in truth . . .

I have known that searching
Where sleeps eludes me
As I hold to sin, or unforgiveness
And long for a life
Uncluttered with grief
Or grudges

Peace—what a word!
We dust pews and marketplaces
Hoping that God wants to be found
That the peace that Jesus breathes
Comes as we wait, even in fear
As we gather, even in unbelief
As we hope against all hope
Long against all longing
And live our lives
Dusting for God's fingerprints
And finding them

. . .

We wait as God in Christ
Dust for our fingerprints,
Pressed into sides split wide
And long—long for days when
We will believe without seeing,
Hope without proof
Testify to what we have seen
And what we have not seen
Heard and not heard
Dusting for fingerprints
All the while

Ronald J. Allen

I began teaching at Christian Theological Seminary in Indianapolis in 1982. When my first research leave arrived in 1990, my greatest need as a teacher with European origins was to become more familiar with African American preaching. Since Henry Mitchell is the dean of African American scholarship in preaching, I asked if I could take the basic class in preaching that he and Ella P. Mitchell offered at the Interdenominational Theological Seminary in Atlanta.[3] They graciously welcomed me, so our household moved to Atlanta for a remarkable year.[4]

The work of Henry Mitchell is foundational scholarship in the history of the African American preaching tradition.[5] Though fresh trends are evolving today, all who interact seriously with the development of African American preaching must take the Mitchell corpus into account.[6] While preachers and scholars of European origin often focus on Professor Mitchell's benchmark analyses of African American preaching, Mitchell sees the core of his trans-rational approach as prescriptive for preaching in any Christian movement. Indeed, Mitchell believes that much preaching in historic churches of European origin is sterile. Eurocentric preaching often drowns in ideas but does not connect with congregations at the deepest levels (feeling and intuition).

On the one hand, I resonate with Professor Mitchell's point with respect to Eurocentric preaching. Hearing such sermons I have sometimes felt like a withered piece of grass blowing across a desert. On the other hand, I do have two questions about Mitchell's approach for congregations of European origin. For one, while Mitchell finds that experiential encounters through preaching override the negative tapes of oppression with which the dominant culture grinds down African Americans, I wonder whether such preaching calibrated to congregations of European origin is powerful enough to reinscribe the tapes of racism, privilege, self-service, and other manifestations of sin that are that are deeply embedded in such congregations. Second, I believe that Mitchell downplays the transformative potential of ideas, at least for some people.[7] To offer my own experience (a pivotal category for Mitchell) as anecdotal evidence: I am often electrified by ideas.

Professor Mitchell shares many perspectives with other writers in the New Homiletic.[8] However, whereas other major voices in the New

Homiletic were often inspired by Eurocentric philosophy and literary theory, Mitchell's perspective arises from his observations about African American experience refined by his study of West African religion, educational theory, psychology, and theology. Mitchell describes his homiletic as "folk generated."[9] As I note shortly, this approach has great methodological potential for Eurocentric preachers.

Majority-culture churches in the long-established denominations in North America have been in institutional decline since the beginning of the New Homiletic. The causes of this diminution are numerous and complicated, but many interpreters think that loss of theological clarity, purpose, and mission are central.[10] A key agenda item for contemporary preaching is to identify a transformative homiletic for the long-established Eurocentric communions.

The work of Henry Mitchell provides a methodological perspective that might help with the task of congregational transformation. One reason that African American preaching is so powerful within that community is that the preaching is fueled by folk culture. Taking a cue from Professor Mitchell, Eurocentric scholars and ministers might explore folk communication in communities of European culture as possible patterns of preaching.[11]

Such an effort would be consistent with developing postmodern approaches to preaching. Proponents of the modern worldview tend to seek universals. While theoreticians and preachers in the New Homiletic have distanced themselves from the hegemony of the rational-propositional approach to preaching, many seem to share modernity's penchant for the universal, especially when they prescribe a particular system of preaching to be used in all congregations.

By contrast, postmodern thinkers emphasize particularity in almost every aspect of life. From this point of view, preachers today should seek forms of preaching that are congruent with the multiple shapes of consciousness and community in the postmodern era. While Professor Mitchell privileges certain qualities of awareness (intuitive and emotive) and expression (inductivity, narrative, and metaphor), he insists that preachers honor diversity in culture and community. Mitchell thus provides an avenue into diverse approaches to preaching that seem better suited to the pluralistic postmodern world.

Moreover, Professor Mitchell may help preachers with authority, one of the most vexing issues of the postmodern church sailing the sea of relativism. For Mitchell, authority emerges in the interplay between the Bible (and Christian tradition and theology) and experience. Tradition and experience both inform and challenge one another. Christian tradition has authority as it is confirmed in liberating experience. Christian tradition often helps name and shape experience. However, neither tradition nor experience is singularly imperial. The sermon becomes authoritative as it serves God's purposes for humankind (for example, reinforcing self-esteem and dignity, reinforcing survival, and bringing about genuine community). Such an approach is welcome in many postmodern communities for it gives a community a place to stand without appealing to arbitrary or oppressive authorities while remaining open to fresh interpretations of tradition and experience.

4

Narrative Renewed

Eugene L. Lowry

My Development of Narrative Preaching— Briefly Noted

I began my formal work in homiletics by coming in through the back door. Four years out of seminary, I transferred into the Missouri West Conference of the United Methodist Church, and was asked to teach adjunctively at Saint Paul School of Theology, in Kansas City. Six years later I was invited to join the faculty. A theologian on the faculty shook my hand as soon as the announcement was made and said, "I want to welcome you formally to Saint Paul School of Theology. I understand that you will be teaching blacksmithing." He did not need to explain what he meant.

For over thirty years now I have been trying to suggest to people that a sermon should move from an *itch* to a *scratch*. As I stated in *The Homiletical Plot*, the most crucial issue with regard to preaching is a sense of discrepancy.[1] No discrepancy, no movement from itch to scratch, probably a muted message!

In that first book, I designed a narrative shape for sermons that could imagine such a movement, involving five steps: upsetting the equilibrium, analyzing the discrepancy, disclosing the clue to resolution, experiencing the gospel, and anticipating the consequences. I thought that I invented that third step, "the principal of reversal," but later I discovered that it had been "stolen" much earlier by Aristotle. And I named the fifth step poorly. When my parents would speak of consequences, it was never a happy day. Instead of talking about anticipating consequences, I should have said anticipating the future—anticipating the future made new by the gospel of Jesus Christ.

Five years later my second book, *Doing Time in the Pulpit*, was published.[2] My principle concern in this work was to say that a sermon is not an object in space but an event in time. The often-used "construction" metaphor for preaching suggests a building image—like what might happen on a corner lot. (It could conjure up pallets and other stuff, with a concrete truck coming into view.) We are thinking space here, even if we do not notice. And when preachers are asked on Thursday about how they are doing with Sunday sermon preparation, we will not be surprised if they say, "I think I'm getting it together." They are utilizing a spatial image rather than a timely image. And it shows in how they "build" their sermon. It was H. Grady Davis who wisely said that if we're going to learn from other arts, we need to learn from the arts that involve a time sequence.[3] Whereas I hoped *Plot* would help people know *how* to shape a narrative sermon, *Doing Time* was an attempt to explain *why* the narrative principle is far more effective in preaching work. *The key principle is that of a plot that involves a strategic delay in the preacher's sermonic meaning.* Other writers have captured the narrative principle in their emphasis upon movement, juxtaposition, conflict, anticipation, phenomenological moves, and telos.

Moreover, in both those first two works, I suggested those occasions when a preacher wisely chooses modifications to the typical plot—adaptations, nuances, differences, options, alternatives. In fact, in *Plot*, the first book, I observed that if you're dealing with a biblical parable or other narrative text, you may not need to create a narrative plot for the sermon because some kind of plot form is already present.

Subsequent writings of mine, such as *How to Preach a Parable* and *The Sermon: Dancing the Edge of Mystery,* offer further options that also honor the narrative principle of plot. For example, *Parable* distinguishes four types of homiletical plots, and *Dancing* enlarges the matter to include other forms of plotted sermons, such as episodal preaching.

With this very brief thumbnail sketch of my writing history, the focus needs now to turn to crucial shifts in communication technology that powerfully have changed the context of the work of preaching, and hence, provide the current challenge that these media shifts pose for us. Finally, we will consider my attempts toward addressing the challenge.

The Screen Revolution

Since 1980, when the first edition of *The Homiletical Plot* was published, the world has been changing dramatically, particularly in terms of media. We are moving from a print to a screen culture. I know this is not received positively by everybody, but the move from book to screen is happening nevertheless—and, as a matter of fact, involves all kinds of screens. This is not to say that the book is dead—anymore than the radio died from the emergence of television. It simply means that it becomes reconfigured within the culture.

My generation finds this shift difficult. Even if one is computer literate, it can be disconcerting. For example, although I am "compatible" with the computer—and used one to write this essay—I still have difficulty reading a book on the monitor, because it has nothing to hold on to, no binding at all! But younger generations have moved from the newspaper to the Internet for news, and from organizational interaction to social networking for personal engagement, even from telephone voice to texting. So, print certainly is still around, but it is finding new modes, new forms.

Note how it is that the *computer screen* has changed our world. It has moved into a position of dominance in the way people interact with and know the world. Recently I was replacing a colleague for a day in a seminary preaching class. There were ten to twelve students there, whom I did not know. Of course, I sought to relate to them. But there was this one man who always had his laptop open in such a way that I saw only his forehead for nearly three hours. I do not know what he looked like at all beneath the forehead and I do not know what he was doing with the computer. I suspect he was playing solitaire, surfing the Internet or instant messaging a friend, but perhaps he was listening and/or even putting memorable notes on the hard drive for safekeeping. It is possible he was ready to Google a question prompted by my input in class. (Google has now become a common verb in our language!) I have no idea what he was doing, but he certainly was not an active participant in class interaction. The computer appeared to grip his attention utterly. He is not alone. After Google and Yahoo! search engines, social networking Web sites like Facebook and video sites like YouTube receive the most hits on the Web. Overall, the computer is the dominant cultural screen—and even trumps television in cultural importance.

The cell phone is now central to interpersonal communication, and note this, we have even turned *cell phones into screens*. The "original" purpose, of course, was to have access to others' voices. But now, texting has transformed the human interaction of cellular use among younger generations. There is a world of difference between hearing a voice and seeing a message, sent by but not personally present to the listener. Further, one of the "advantages" of texting is that you can send a text message while other people think you are doing something else—such as listening to a sermon!

Now, of course, the cell also connects us to the Internet, increasing further the enormity of the computer's power in shaping the way we relate to the world and to one another. This ongoing communicational revolution is both culturally comprehensive and amazingly quick. Moreover, computer-mediated news, both worldwide and local, goes not far before asking for everybody's blogging responses. I want to retort that I do not care what others may be saying, thinking that they ought to "get a life," and then I wonder, "Why am I reading them?"

When the discussion returns to our current preaching context, it will be important to ask what impact "sound bite" text communication might have upon the sermon. Moreover, what does human communication now actually mean?

Of course, there is *television—the older screen*, dating back to World War II. When I first proposed my narrative approach in the 1980s, I relied heavily on television in my teaching for the purpose of narrative modeling. It was enormously helpful because many of the most popular shows had the kind of simple narrative plot line that could be utilized in helping students unaccustomed to narrative categories discover how in fact to shape a sermonic plot. I had three really favorite ones—the first one was *Quincy*.

Quincy was the TV pathologist whose job it was to figure out why people died and who made them die. The plot of the show was often driven by the dynamic that the more Quincy hunted the less he found. Pretty soon he would hit a stone wall (of course) and there would be nothing more that he could do. Absolutely frustrated, finally he would jump off the cliff of reason and do something seemingly incredibly stupid. But when he hit the bottom, there was some serendipitous miracle waiting there for him. He didn't create it, he didn't find it, but it got revealed to him somehow in his frustration. Lying on his back, looking like an absolute idiot, he always discovered whatever it was that fell out of the sky to meet him. He knew then that he had indeed been found, and with it the clue to the case's successful resolution. Well, such chaos is often the case for the preacher's work for next Sunday's sermon.

Sometime (generally early), between Monday and Saturday, preachers get lost and frustrated with the text's primary issue. But *Quincy* helps them observe that the chaos between Monday and Sunday is seldom a detour. It may be the shortest route to resolution for Sunday's message. Because until we suspend, at least temporarily, the orthodoxy that controls how we live our theological lives—until that assumption gets pushed aside, we may not find a new potential resolution born of the gospel. Truth is, we may be trapped in the quicksand of eisegesis, rather than being open to exegesis. In fact, I just have to confess that the Holy Spirit has great trouble trying to get through my deeply held convictions. The Spirit is more likely to have access at the point of my uncertainties, and a little chaos might just provide the avenue that opens an unnoticed door toward Sunday's message.

The second television show I used was *Columbo*. Some of you will remember the detective in the trench coat there in the Arizona sun in the middle of summer, 110 degrees. He would stand next to the pool asking apparently inane questions of people whose answers appeared equally inane. With Quincy we did not know the answer any more than he did, but with Columbo we always knew more. We had seen the crime committed or knew who did it or how they did it. But he had not a clue. The enjoyment in watching that show—in which we already knew the conclusion—hinged on both our sense of privileged position, and that we did not know *how* it was that Columbo would find out the data he needed.

It was amazing how Columbo with the trench coat and the inane questions was able to sense stuff—feel it, hear it, smell it, see it, taste it. He was able in his ignorance to discover more than we in our knowledge were able to do. You remember how it was, his backing out of the critical scene, about to leave the interview with cigar in hand. Suddenly, he would turn around and say, "Oh, one more question . . ." And we knew that would be the critical question, the clincher to solve the case, but we did not know why, *even after he asked it*, said thank you, and departed. And to think we already knew so much more than he, but yet couldn't quite figure out what key evidence he found, until later he would let us all know. How could we have missed it?

I used *Columbo* to try to help students learn how to help hearers experience discrepancy in the sermon, how to linger, how never to pass a moment without stopping to notice what others might miss. For example, whenever Paul wrote a letter to a church, he would always start off by saying something like, "I thank God for you all, for your faith is known in all the world." You have heard it—it happened in Romans, in all the Corinthian correspondence, and all the rest. But when you read the opening of Galatians, do not pass the opening litany without noticing the difference. In Galatians, Paul did not thank them for anything. Instead, he said, "I am astonished that you are so quickly deserting the one who called you in the grace of Christ and are turning to a different gospel" (Gal. 1:6). Linger there a moment. Why would he not find something nice to say—particularly if he was about to blurt out such an accusation as he did? Linger awhile just like Columbo always lingered. Look around, listen to the context, hear the attitude. There may be a discrepancy that walks up to meet you. This strategy is particularly important with passages we know all too well.

The third TV show I utilized was *The Dukes of Hazzard*. I had students who would not admit that they watched it, but it followed the homiletical plot in all the stages—and often crudely enough that it was easy to notice, and hence from which it was easy to learn. It was not exactly fine art—all the better for catching what the writer is doing. There was never much gospel to it, of course, but it had the plot right there. When the Dodge Charger was just about to arrive at the county line, and Bo and Luke suddenly realized that the real action was back on Main Street, that

Dodge Charger would perform a quick 180-degree turn, and you could see the dust coming up. The turn was never done on a highway, never done on concrete, always in the dirt—and it would spin around. You could put a little caption at the bottom of the screen when the Dodge Charger did it. It would read, "The principle of reversal."

For two decades television was assisting me in showing students how sermonic plots work. We had these nice simple plots. Hollywood and I were on the same page. But then new shows began popping up on the television screen that pushed the narrative envelope dramatically.

M*A*S*H was one of the early ones. Here we had a hospital show that was altogether different than those earlier doctor shows. This was no *Marcus Welby, M.D.* In *M*A*S*H* injured soldiers provided the ongoing action of the show and continued to undergird the theme of constant care regardless of the eccentricities of the medical personalities. Central to the plot, however, was the *ongoing relationship* of all the major characters. Gone was the earlier type of TV offerings that typically consisted of a singular thirty-minute plot—with beginning, middle, and end. Here the patients were important but not central to the ongoing plot. Some lived, some died, many left their mark, but the staff stayed on with their mission. The interaction of the main characters week after week was the plot's central focus—together with the constancy of its antiwar theme. Overall, TV plots were taking on greater complexity of plot and subplots.

Then came *NYPD Blue*—with a similar plot structure between the subplots of people who would appear and then disappear in an episode or two and, on the other hand, the central interactive police characters. And now we have *Grey's Anatomy*, and I want to know: In *Grey's Anatomy*, who's sick here—the patients or the staff?

Similarly, there was recently *Boston Legal*, again with a much more complicated plot line than earlier television typically provided. Well, here you had a little communion at the end providing the chance for reflection. But it wasn't bread and wine—the wine was there but the bread was replaced with a couple cigars. Instead, what you noticed about *Boston Legal* was a ceaseless wave of cases and attorney relations. The wave changed slowly. The multiple levels of subplots across numerous episodes served the larger ongoing relationship of the lawyers Alan and Denny. It is worth noting that the program never brought to conclusion all the cases that were pending.

At least one case would be left hanging—providing plenty of itches to bring us back next week. The relationships continued to grow and evolve across time. By contrast, Perry Mason's relationship with Della never changed. Screens are using narratives differently these days.

Clearly, such contemporary television offerings are not so easily catalogued or accessed as models for preachers working on next week's sermon. At the same time, the life of the congregation in general and the movement of the liturgy on a particular Sunday does indeed provide the kind of ongoing complexity that has important connections with today's television programming. But the question is, How do all these media variations have an impact on the Sunday sermonic plot, or should they?

Of course, one of the biggest shifts in more recent television programming is the reality show. It joins the television sports programming, by means of a process that features the so-called American gospel, namely, that "anyone can do it if they have a mind to." Yet, what is presented is the reverse, namely that the bottom line reinforces the reality that the losers are many and the winners are few. But unlike other forms of radio and TV, with some reality shows the viewers actually determine the bottom line.

Of course, the screens that are upstaging the book or supplementing print are not only in our office or living room. There is also the great big screen that has been borrowed from the boardroom and the classroom and has been placed in the church chancel. Some of us may not like the *chancel screen*, but we better get used to it. It is here to stay. And, although there are numerous problems with the chancel screen, in fact, some forms of its utilization are good, even powerful. Of course, many find the presence of a screen a distraction in the liturgical setting—even out of place. But if we were to imagine the scene following the Guttenberg revolution, there had to be many who objected to books in the holy place. The printing press with movable type changed all that! Now another technological revolution is happening with what will surely have a remarkable impact.

There are significant positive uses for the sanctuary screen. The corporate body of Christ may be gathering on a particular Sunday, and be greeted with a video projection of church youth on the mission trip. Maybe it is in DVD motion or maybe a set of CD pictures, but there you see people you know, and children of people you know, all present, leading the gathering for worship. Such a video projection participates, is embodied, in the liturgical plot.

At Velda Rose United Methodist Church in Mesa, Arizona, they have had as many as three thousand in attendance when the snowbirds come south for the winter. These worshipers tend to be older people, many of whom are not used to screens in worship in their hometowns. On the screens are projected the hymns as they are sung. Although the bulletin reveals hymnal page numbers, most look to the screen to follow the words to the already familiar hymns. The vitality of hymn singing at that congregation has changed remarkably, because now they are looking up instead of down.

Recently, a funeral service was held for a prominent middle-aged member of Asbury United Methodist Church in Phoenix who had died of cancer. During the church service the pastor told the congregation that before the woman's death he had asked her what biblical text was particularly important in empowering her for the journey she was traveling. The pastor then named the chapter and verses of her favorite scriptural passage, and announced to the congregation: "Why don't we hear her read the text." And immediately a video recording was projected upon the screen of her reading the passage—recorded a couple months prior to her death.

At the same time screens are not beneficial if they only divert; screens should undergird. For example, screen use can diminish the power of the read Scripture. It is my fairly common experience as a guest preacher that projecting the written passage on the screen becomes counterproductive. Rather than the moment being an important point of initial connection between preacher and congregation (particularly if the reading occurs immediately prior to the sermon itself), the screen gets the connection with the congregation instead, and the congregation's task of following the printed text preempts the power of orality—its inflection, emphasis, and nuance. Indeed, in this context, print on screen may sabotage the embodiment of the Word. Rather than the congregation reading the text on the screen, it would be better to show the actual reading of the text, so that the screen supports the public reading instead of turning everyone into private readers.

It is helpful to remember that there is a powerful difference between what you see and what you hear. In some circumstances, *seeing* takes precedence over *hearing*. For example, one might remember a congregational leader trying to convince the church board to approve a formal resolution for some expensive mission opportunity, who had carefully developed and rehearsed a powerful speech to persuade the board to commit the money necessary for the project. But before the powerful speech began, a printed fact sheet was distributed. Bad timing it was, because the eyes moved to the page and stopped the ears from hearing the powerful speech. In the end everyone knew the numbers, but wondered about the logic of the request.

Yet, we should not be fooled into dismissing the opposite possibility—when the power of orality rules over the visual—particularly when stimulating the imagination and the will is at stake. In this situation, it is helpful to remember that what you see is *out there*, what you hear is *in here*; one is exterior, the other interior.

Elsewhere I have spoken about my experience of *The Lone Ranger* on radio when I was a child. I remember hearing the "William Tell Overture" as the Lone Ranger rode away on Silver. My imagination was focused on the horse. Oh, what a mammoth animal that was! What a steed! "Hi Ho, Silver . . . Away!" Powerful! But then, a generation later I was walking through the living room where my children were watching *The Lone Ranger* on TV. I could not believe the puny pony that showed up and claimed to be Silver! That mule should have been retired years earlier!

The key here, of course, is that television's horse was defined, while my childhood's Silver on radio was birthed in my soul. In attempted participation with TV's image, there was little opportunity for real engagement. Indeed, it is often the case that the eye's visual reception is flat, and no match for the engagement of radio's orality for the ear. Marshall McLuhan would say television's horse was hot, and radio's horse was cool—and opened the door for participation.

Given the emergence of screen utilization in many congregational worship settings, new considerations need to be formed with regard to effective use—liturgically and homiletically. For example, evaluation of the power of CD and DVD utilization surely suggests both positively valuable opportunities, such as the funeral service described above, as well as negatively experienced counterproductive situations—such as when a movie clip inside a sermon serves to derail the sermonic plot. Often some of the congregation who have seen the movie will continue on to the film's next remembered scene, while others who have not seen the film will wonder where next the film might have gone—detouring what the preacher hoped to accomplish by the film's use. I have heard several pastors remark about how they now use fewer film clips than before for precisely the reasons just now mentioned. Otherwise put, when a film clip prompts imagination, typically it *controls* the subject, whereas when the sermonic oral description of a scene *prompts* imagination, the preacher's intent is more likely to determine the direction of thought.

The influence of the screen in our culture and our worship services raises again a tension that was part of the early discussion of the New Homiletic. Whether it is a computer monitor, cell phone texting, the television, or projected images and words in worship, there is a tension of critical proportions here. It is the ongoing and ever-changing tension between orality and textuality, between the human voice and print, between time and space, between event and instruction, between what we hear and what we see.

Indeed, it is interesting that in many worship services that use screens you will find a bulletin with the listing of the congregational liturgical experience, perhaps followed by numerous announcements. And then, by page 3, you find a heading that says "Sermon Notes." All in attendance are instructed to fill in the blanks in the form *while listening to the sermon*—to make sure they remember what they heard. (In one congregation I visited the bulletin gave statistics about how little you remember of what you hear.)

Can you imagine someone coming up to you in a shopping mall and saying, "Did I ever hear a good one. What a side-splitter! You're going to love this. By the way, have you got a pencil and pad? I'd like you to take notes so you don't forget it." Well, if you take notes, you might or might not remember the joke, but certainly you will not laugh at the punch line. Memorization is not the point of a joke. Evocation is.

In the context of preaching, focusing on memory retention is to rob the hearers of the immediacy of *experiencing* the gospel proclaimed. Memory retention is not the central focus of the sermonic goal. The focus is creative engagement with the Word. The goal is not communicating information but, as Charles Rice suggests in a reference to Dorothy Sayers, it is the linkage of recognition and revelation. "The act of preaching," notes Walter

Brueggemann, "is not instruction, rational discourse, or moral suasion. It is the invitation and permit to practice a life of doxology and obedience."[4] Or, as Henry Mitchell reminds us, a sermon must have a behavioral goal. Citing the primacy of the oral, he warns us over and over against the bondage of transliteralism. We need to remember that, as Walter Ong put it, "Print encourages a sense of closure."[5] Print is comfortable only with finality. That is why we ought to get nervous when hearing a preacher talk about "writing" a sermon.

To make "writing the sermon" the goal of the preparation process is inadvertently to trade sermonic focus from orality to print. And likely it will have a negative effect on the sermon as preached. Whether it is by "writing" the sermon, projecting parts of the text of the sermon on screen, or having the congregation create an outline of the sermon in the bulletin, to submit the oral/aural, timely event of the sermon to the strictures of the screen/print method of communicating is to cheat the sermon of some of its expected power. It sacrifices the way the mode of orality clusters ideas and images by association that engage the mind and heart by turning the sermon into literality-based organization. Unfortunately, ideas in oral form for the ear to hear are transposed into print on a page for the eye to follow. Shaping the movement of the oral form is a more conducive way to imagine sermon preparation.

Having briefly described my ongoing work in the field of narrative preaching and the challenge of the screen revolution as experienced on television, computer, cell phone and in liturgical practice, it now is time to ask, "How have I responded to these challenges and how might we continue to respond?"

Updating the Narrative Model of Preaching

When I consider my core narrative approach with nearly thirty years of development, I note several shifts worth observing.

First, with greater clarity of hindsight I note, for example, that although my doctorate was focused on aesthetic epistemology, the language of my first writing, *The Homiletical Plot*, was couched in discursive categories. For example, I called the second stage of the narrative plot "analyzing the discrepancy." That seems more like my intercollegiate debate work of the

1950s than my writing in the late '70s. "Analyzing the discrepancy" is accurate language if you are preaching a logical, rational sort of sermon. That is the reason why, in later writings, I changed the name of the second sermonic stage to "complication." Moreover, David Schlafer was enormously helpful in naming three basic strategies for carrying the thread of thought through the five stages of the narrative plot—namely *argument, image,* and *story.* "Analyzing the discrepancy" only makes sense of the first one of these. "Image" and "story" are more likely to involve aesthetic categories of knowing.

Second, the radical "reversal" or "sudden shift" does not always happen to occur as I suggested originally—that is, after "complication" and prior to "experiencing the gospel." That's the way it works in the parable of the Prodigal Son. The son is willing to consider his father to be dead in order to get his inheritance—*Oops,* conflict. Then he loses the whole inheritance—*Ugh,* complication. He then turns back home—*Aha,* disclosing the clue to resolution. He is graciously received by his father—*Whee,* experience of the gospel. And finally, he is restored to sonship—*Yeah,* anticipating the future. That follows the narrative plot—1,2,3,4,5—nicely. But this is not always the case. Take the story of the healing of Bartimaeus. He gets healed *first* (experiencing the gospel), then the radical shift (reversal) happens. In short, sometimes the good news happens *just before* the turn, sometimes it *is the turn,* sometimes it is *just after the turn.* Sometimes the plot goes 1-2-3-4-5, sometimes it goes 1-2-4-3-5, other times it may go 1-2-3/4-5.

Third, while *The Homiletical Plot* worked with great appreciation for Fred Craddock's transforming work, *As One without Authority,* all subsequent writings of mine have turned also to the work of other colleagues—particularly the other scholars featured in this volume—whose fine contributions both confirm and challenge my ideas. There are Mitchell's eyewitness account, Rice's story, Buttrick's moves, and Craddock's inductive strategy. Yet, the category of the homiletical theory known as "the New Homiletic" includes many more than these five. Understanding that there is great diversity among us, nonetheless, we have enough in common to be linked together, both by friend and foe alike. We may not all be on the same page but we certainly are all in the same chapter.

Perhaps the centerpiece of our commonality has to do with our concern for strategic narrative process. My way of identifying a narrative sermon has been to say that such a sermon involves a strategic delay in the preacher's meaning. Thus, in my most recent book, *The Sermon: Dancing the Edge of Mystery*, I shifted from the term *narrative* to the term *plotted* as descriptive of such sermons.

Finally, in relation to changes the screen presents in our culture and churches, I believe the kind of plotted or narrative preaching that needs to be better developed theoretically is the one that in *The Sermon* I called the *episodal sermon*. By "episodal" I mean the type of sermons I have noticed cropping up among late boomers, a type of sermon that does not directly follow the steps I have utilized in identifying my version of narrative preaching, but that are nonetheless narrative in shape. In this type of sermon, the preacher develops a chain of vignettes, episodes, or scenes. I do not mean the kind of sermon that just strings together anecdote after anecdote without connection, but one in which the episodes are shaped in such a way that tension grows although the unity may be hidden until the final turn is achieved. The sermonic evocation happens by means of the unity revealed.

This is not unlike some of the classic preaching of Fred Craddock. He may begin by exploring a biblical text, similar in form to other preachers. But then, all of a sudden, he jumps out of the text before there is any kind of resolution, and without announcing the shift about to happen. He just jumps to aisle nine in our local supermarket. We don't know why, but we know Fred knows why, and it is all right because we are with Fred and in good time we, too, shall know why. What we do know is that obviously there is something about the text that is not quite finished *and* that somehow will relate to aisle nine. Sure enough, Fred very shortly is going to share what it is that he has spotted in aisle nine that we have missed for twenty years. All of a sudden he is exploring another text, and then on to another scene. Finally, it dawns on us: "That's it, that's it!" And we look up at Fred only to find that Fred is already seated behind the pulpit. He never gives us the last line. We say the last line that is now so clear. Well, that is episodal at its best.

Tex Sample does something similar. He tells a story and moves on, leaving one asking, "Does that mean what I think? Surely that's it, but his eyes suggest that it may be more important than that." Better listen on. And then Tex will enter into some discursive material for awhile, give another story or two, and when he gets to the end of the last story, finally we all understand fully what the first story meant. The sermon is filled with short episodes, but as a whole it is a sweep toward unity and evocation.

Powerfully, Tom Troeger illustrated episodal preaching in an actual wedding sermon manuscript in *Imagining a Sermon*. Contrasting what he described as a "rhetorical sermon for the print generation" with a sermon "for the mass media generation," he covers the same theological content, but with one sermon utilizing a deductive explanatory structure and the other featuring an episodal form of three imagined anniversary scenes.[6] The difference is immense.

Moreover, David Buttrick's work has been episodal all along. Utilizing five or six "moves" (with strict rules about what you can and cannot do in them), the goal is to shape a corporate consciousness of some aspect of the gospel. Some other forms of episodal preaching could be characterized as involving a "loose narrative" shape, rather than the more tightly shaped linear thought lines of my model. Episodal narrative preaching tends to "turn" *without* explicitly signaling the turn. On the other hand, Buttrick's model seems to me to be in between these two similar forms of narrative preaching in that although there is no explicit rationale given for the move to the next "move," nonetheless, there exists some kind of implicit linear connection.

Episodal preaching as a category of narrative homiletics is, I believe, particularly important for our time—although it has little explicit literature written to date. The reason for its named identification here is that other contexts of communication in our time and culture also lean toward the episodal. The multiplicity of subplots running underneath a major plot in current television programming, described above, is clearly following episodal form. *Boston Legal* is a good example. Current jazz improvisational forms dance vertically around the harmonic structures, rather than moving horizontally around the forward motion of the melody. Even text conversation without actual presence (like note passing in junior high English classes of old, when you could gather your own balance before responding) has an episodal feel to it.

The danger of this tendency in our time, of course, is fragmentation, perhaps even as bad as living by sound bites. And what does this mean about metanarratives involving alphas and omegas? Yet, what is clear in the wide range of this continuum is *narrative time*. What is less clear is to what unfortunate degree textuality is winning over orality in our culture, and how badly has lectionary practice moved preaching from proclamation to informational instruction.

Martin Luther had it right. Faith is an acoustical affair, and I think the preaching office will profit by continuing to pursue a new hearing.

Responses

Dale P. Andrews

The concept of "a renewed homiletic" really should have been considered originally when developing the work of inductive methodologies in those texts of the mid-twentieth century. The work of such authors as H. Grady Davis, David James Randolph, and Fred Craddock in dramatic ways broke through dominant propositional and deductive forms of preaching in Western mainline church traditions. This work then broadened immediately the scope of inductive preaching into brilliant treatments of the preaching event as encounter, narrative strategies, experience and meaning-making, hearers' participation, and pedagogy. And we are deeply indebted!

I confess that I am rather amazed, however, that the misguided claims of originality in the ascription of "the New Homiletic" prevails. The expansive practices of inductive preaching methods have been generationally nurtured and apprenticed in more oral traditions, and quite predominantly cultivated in black preaching. My hope is that most of the authors of this assumed "New Homiletic," who have been invited to reflect on their work in this volume, would illumine the ways this nomenclature is not only mistaken, but also missed pedagogical possibilities in the absence of significant attention to the more oral traditions of homiletics, like black preaching. Actually, I propose that Richard Eslinger's concept of a "New Hearing" be adopted as a more reflective gauge marking this mid-twentieth-century movement in homiletics; therefore, this current volume might be more effectively entitled "A Re(New)ed Hearing." Within such a hearing, I would like to reflect on Eugene Lowry's rather insightful understanding of narrative designs for preaching in light of this broadened scope of renewing homiletics, ending with attention to his projections for renewing narrative methodology and relevant pedagogy.

Lowry understands that one of his own early developments beyond his initial treatment of "the homiletical plot" was to embrace the sermon as an event in time. In his development of narrative preaching, Lowry notes that H. Grady Davis conceived of sermons in the stream of time. One may think initially that sermons are of course a moment in the flow of life or the unfolding time span of congregational life. With others, Davis argued for preaching to create a hearing of the gospel as God moving in both the past and the present.[7] But for the experience of a preaching event itself, time has another intricate character, which is experienced within or through the sermon. Lowry's work masterfully nurtures the sense of plotted strategy in the delayed resolution of some challenge or problem engaged through the sermon. For Davis, the concept of time here has everything to do with creating a hearing. It is a performance conveying or, rather, nurturing an experience of the message.[8]

The future activity of God's self-revelation in the lives of our hearers meets with the past of God's activity in a current experience of God's agency in the sermon time itself. Similarly, James Earl Massey regarded the preaching event as a "happening."[9] The happening is not simply a passive experience for our hearers. This new hearing in homiletics stresses in multiple ways the convergence of "what the sermon does" and "what the hearers experience" in the preaching event. David Randolph related the new hermeneutics movement in the academy to this happening and encounter within preaching.[10] This convergence calls upon the preacher's discernment and preparation of the sermon in light of one's anticipation of the hearers' participation.

Lowry's turn to communication technology and media illustrates dramatically, I believe, this convergence of discernment and preparation with anticipation and participation. The plot is experienced as a discrepancy, but even more so a chaos in which we encounter the agency of God meeting us in the chaos. Lowry uses the hearers' experiences of plotted narratives in media to help preachers discern how to shape narrativity in their sermons. Like in black preaching traditions, church cultures have for generations shaped storytelling in preaching with the oral structures of biblical narratives and experience. What we learn from such inherited traditions is that the event of communication in preaching is integrally part of the preacher's discernment, preparation, and sermon construction directly. The added challenge of media and technology for preaching, then, still requires us to nurture the convergence of "what the sermon does" and "what the hearers experience" in the preaching event.

Lowry extends his use of television media to consider newer genres like the so-called reality shows. Here, too, the convergence of genre and event weighs both passive and active participation within the encounter. In his recent text, *The Sermon: Dancing the Edge of Mystery*, Lowry underscores a fundamental insight within a kerygmatic "new hearing" in the sermon as an encounter involving the hearers' lives and participation.[11] While Lowry seems mistakenly to reduce much of black preaching in the new hearing to an earlier conception in Henry Mitchell's work, called "transconscious" congregational or even generational communication,[12] Lowry does extend his treatment of the new hearing into what James Cone later called "a poetic happening, an evocation of an indescribable reality in the lives of people."[13] Lowry also notes that Randolph picked up on evocation when trying to name the new hearing. Unfortunately, Randolph did not develop how oral traditions like black preaching have cultivated evocation. Lowry helpfully turns to the "art of evocation," albeit again without the continued dialogue with these more inductive cultures of preaching traditions themselves. Still, his work here should not be dismissed even with this problem in tow. He sees the interconnectedness of the sermon event with the lived experiences of one's hearers and the actual experiences within the sermon event. Lowry critically observes how the anticipation and participation in the preaching event can reflect an ideational experience within an encounter shaped throughout the worship service, but revealed dramatically in the preaching task.[14]

Black preaching traditions have developed these concepts within intricate mentoring methods of pedagogy comprising apprenticeship practices of learning preaching within church praxis. The encounter between constructive communication and experiential listening is central to the tasks of anticipation and participation between the preacher and hearers. A preacher both anticipates and seeks an encounter with God's self-revealing Word in sermon preparation. Yet the tasks of anticipation also include the discerned activity of revelation for the sermon event in the context of the hearers' lives and actual listening experience. Of course, the hearers also anticipate the sermon in view of experiencing a preaching event. This encounter within the sermon's preparation guides the construction of sermons anticipating how to recreate the encounter for the participation of hearers. The hearers' participation reflects their own encounter, which in essence is the preacher's reconstructed encounter, or an anticipated reencounter. Indispensable, however, to the process is openness to this reencounter being transformed still by the hearers' participation in the preaching event. This openness, in turn, has been central to Fred Craddock's work within the new hearing of inductive preaching,[15] not at all distinct from many folk traditions like black preaching praxis that have refined mentoring practices for learning preaching. These practices reflect the encounter–reencounter exchange in that they press induction into the pedagogical process of preaching ministry.

Teaching preaching and sermon preparation constructs communication for the preaching event in anticipating the experiential listening of hearers and how their participation will help to shape the sermon event into their own discernment and encounter with divine revelation. I have argued elsewhere that whether one refers to induction, narrative preaching, storytelling, phenomenological experience, a happening, a move, immediate experience within the sermon's development, or hearers' responses and participation, the "new hearing" movement of homiletics mirrors black preaching traditions. I believe the various forms of pedagogy from folk traditions, such as black preaching apprenticeship, offer an important development of homiletic methodology and perhaps a potential "renewed hearing"—a task that translates the mentor-apprentice models of black preaching into more accessible cross-cultural pedagogy for the homiletic classroom.

Lowry's work on narrative strategies similarly extends his earlier work into pedagogy for dominant forms of experiential listening now emerging amidst changing technology and the consequent forms of episodal encounter, which he extrapolates from Lucy Rose's treatment of conversational preaching.[16] Lowry's turn to episodal preaching requires further pedagogical development in homiletics to guide potential preachers into inductive movements within sermon time, as Lowry had stressed with Grady Davis, but with attention to the multiplicity of episodes and the multitasking character of contemporary culture increasingly shaped by communication technology.

Here, however, I believe Grady's turn to "dramatic continuity" will be a more useful recovery to Lowry than the more typically referenced organic form to "inductive continuity," since the former stresses the complication and resolution components so central to Lowry's work, but still requires constructive methods for weaving episodes into the unity Lowry rightly underscores. The renewed hearing Lowry illumines may be in need of something other than the Hegelian synthesis Davis concedes. Hence, methods for constructing a unifying plot running as undertow to the tides of select episodes will require our continued efforts to expand the new hearing and pedagogy for our hearers' experiential participation in the preaching event. And in this call, Lowry has done well to renew some of our narrative strategies for another generation of preaching!

Eunjoo Mary Kim

Among contemporary homileticians, Eugene L. Lowry's contribution to the New Homiletic is immeasurable. His first and historic work, *The Homiletical Plot*, is a groundbreaking book in the field of preaching, providing a new, transformational style of preaching, which is a movement "from an itch to a scratch," with clarity and creativity. In his later works, Lowry shows how he has tirelessly tried to evolve his genius idea of the homiletical plot. In his latest book, *The Sermon: Dancing the Edge of Mystery*, Lowry proposes "the episodal sermon" as one of the narrative shapes. According to him, the episodal sermon is a type in which "the preacher develops a chain of vignettes, episodes, or scenes." The distinctive process of the episodal sermon, says Lowry,

> may appear to jump almost thoughtlessly from one vignette to another seemingly unrelated one—until the intentional internal logic is exposed. How different from the narrative sermon, which moves with increased tension until there is a final release born of the sudden shift. Likely, the episodal sermon is much more laid-back . . . the modality may involve more wonderment than the grip of tension.[17]

In his essay here, Lowry emphasizes the significance of the episodal sermon in relation to our contemporary culture. As he rightly points out, we are living in a changing culture influenced by the advancement of communication technology; it is crucial for contemporary preachers to realize the shift from a print culture to a screen culture and its significant impact on our congregational lives. The computer, the television, the cellular phone, video projections, and other media have challenged our Sunday worship and preaching styles as well as shifted our everyday communicational methods. If our goal for preaching is to make "creative engagement with the Word," as Lowry suggests, we must take seriously the issue of how to develop a more conducive and effective style of preaching appealing to this changing congregational culture.

Lowry reaffirms the significance of the plot and orality of a sermon in relation to our screen culture and convinces us that the episodal sermon is one of the most appropriate narrative types for our contemporary secular and church cultures. While Lowry limits his exploration of the episodal sermon to shaping or plotting a sermon, its basic movement that each vignette or story is "seemly unrelated" and that "the unity may be hidden until the final turn is achieved" challenges the preacher to think of preaching outside of the box and to go further with that movement to create new approaches to preaching.

Following are some of my homiletical insights gained from Lowry's episodal sermon that, I hope, can contribute to the renewed homiletic for the future of the preaching ministry. The first insight that I gained from Lowry's episodal sermon is flexibility of preaching style. The shape of the episodal sermon can be modified to a variety of different preaching types. For example, my proposal of "the spiral form,"[18] based on the Asian way of indirect communication, is illustrative of the episodal sermon. Another example is to include a few mini-sermons (or homilies) in the event of preaching. Considering that the Revised Common Lectionary is now popular among mainline denominational churches, the texts assigned for the Sunday in the RCL can be used in creating mini-sermons from different perspectives under the unified theme of the preaching on a Sunday worship service. More precisely, the preacher can prepare a pair or a sequel of sermons with two or three mini-sermons rather than one full-length sermon from the lectionary texts. They will be "seemingly unrelated" but will eventually be unified toward one theme. Between mini-sermons, an intermission can be provided as a time for reflection with music or other liturgical elements.

The second insight emerging from the concept of the episodal sermon is that preaching should be a synthetic performance. As Lowry stresses in his essay, the episodal sermon is based on images, stories, and scenes rather than on the logic of argument. In other words, the episodal sermon is aesthetic. It can be best delivered through a synthetic performance, which requires not only the preacher's voice with modulation but also her kinesthetic movements and facial expressions. Like in a drama or a movie, background pictures on the sanctuary screen, props and lighting, and sound and musical effects at specific moments of the performance will be effective tools for the congregation to experience the spoken words.

Moreover, like other performances, the preaching of the episodal sermon requires deliberate preparation and practice. Although Lowry seems to devalue a writing stage during the preparation for preaching by contrasting orality and textuality, it is important to remember that actors and actresses strenuously try to memorize and internalize their scripts rather than speaking randomly and promptly. Similarly, it is necessary for the preacher to both prepare and perform a qualitative script that is a written oral form, rather than a manuscript or a note. Through the artistic performance, the dead letters in the script will become alive, and the congregation will engage with the living words.

The understanding of preaching as a synthetic performance leads us to the third homiletical insight that preaching is a team ministry or a shared ministry. If we want to practice the episodal sermon as a synthetic performance, it is virtually impossible for the preacher to do that alone. Preaching should no longer be understood as the journey of a lone star. Instead, it should be a collaborative teamwork. The preacher may organize a sermon committee, including church staff and laypeople who are interested and talented in assisting the ministry of preaching. They are supposed to help the preacher not only prepare a sermon by studying the biblical text together and scripting and dramatizing a sermon, but also participate in its performance with the preacher. For example, preaching a pair of mini-sermons can be shared with a member of the sermon committee rather than having the preacher do both. The role of the sermon committee can be extended to giving constructive sermon feedback on a regular basis as well as preparing and performing a sermon.

Finally, Lowry's awareness of the advancement of communication technology reminds us that our context for preaching is not limited to its local context. We are living in a global web of interconnectedness. Through the Internet, we receive overflowing information about the reality of human lives locally and globally. Furthermore, many churches are benefited by the technology of the Internet to share their worship services and preaching by posting a sermon manuscript or a videocast on their Web sites. Therefore, preaching is not limited to the targeted local congregation but is heard or read by the unknown audience of the virtual community beyond its geographical boundaries. In addition, it is noteworthy that congregations in North America experience multicultural and multiracial environments not only through the Internet, but also in their real lives in their churches as well as in society. In this web of interconnectedness, whose story will be included and whose story will be excluded in the episodal sermon? Whose perspective will be respected and whose perspective will be ignored? Indeed, the future of the preaching ministry demands that the preacher critically reflect on such unprecedented questions emerging from our changing context for preaching.

Homiletic *Renewed*

David Buttrick

A t the beginning of my *Homiletic* there's a fib. A bare-faced lie. In the preface I say I had planned to write chapters on "Preaching and Worship" as well as chapters on "Preaching in the Social World." A deliberate lie. Fact is, I did not *plan*, I actually *wrote* a 350-page volume with all those chapters and more. But *Homiletic* was quite long enough. So guess what, we chucked the book, we tossed an entire volume. Actually, it is rather exhilarating to throw out a book; you learn your precious words are not indispensable. Nonetheless, you all should be grateful; *Homiletic* is thick enough as is. My impudent wife says that when you have finished reading the book, it will make a great doorstop. So much for reminiscence.

A Humpty-Dumpty Culture

Now let's take a look at the "New Homiletic." There are five of us gathered in this volume, all who have done different things. 1970 was the banner year: Fred Craddock wrote *As One without Authority* urging inductive preaching; Henry Mitchell produced his hugely important *Black Preaching*; and Charles Rice published *Interpretation and Imagination*, a book on preaching and contemporary literature. Then in 1980, with colleagues, Charles Rice issued *Preaching the Story* and Eugene Lowry, *The Homiletical Plot*, both books promoting forms of narrative preaching. Then in 1987, I tagged along to confuse everyone with the word *phenomenology*.[1] The books do different things, but notice they were all written during a two-decade period, the 1970s and the 1980s, as the curtain was tumbling on a five-hundred-year epoch. They are a literature on the cusp, scribbled at the weary end of an age, because suddenly in the 1990s everyone started chattering about being "postmodern." Maybe reality finally caught up with us and we noticed our world had changed. Clearly, the New Homiletic was the product of a particular waning age but, at best, was trying to tiptoe toward an emerging future.

Looking backward, cultural historians mark the modern age as beginning around 1500 with the Renaissance and the Reformation. The epoch has been labeled "The Enlightenment" by most historians, though theologian Paul Tillich tagged the same period "The Protestant Era." For church historians, the Reformation began when burly Martin Luther shouted, "Here I stand, I cannot do otherwise," while testifying before the Diet of Worms.[2] But for most historians, the key figure is René Descartes who dreamed "a marvelous science," chanting *cogito ergo sum*, "I think, therefore I am."[3] Listen again to the two men, Luther and Descartes: "Here I stand" and "I think, therefore I am." Both men began with a personal pronoun, both engaged in skeptical thinking, and both employed objective reason in science and in theology. For five hundred years, Western culture patched together objective reason and personal faith. But, finally, in the twentieth century the patch tore and "Enlightenment" ended in a split disarray—objective/subjective, social/personal, reason/feeling. How can we put a Humpty-Dumpty culture back together again?

Rethinking Revelation

Let's move from the distant past and stumble toward our own time; all of us here were born in the twentieth century. So narrow the lens, sharpen focus, and let's look at our own lifetime. At the start of the twentieth century, there were two great fields of study, hard sciences and an emerging new science of the self, psychology. And both fields seemed to threaten Christian certainty. For centuries, Christian theologians had spoken of *general revelation* and *special revelation.* What was general revelation? The notion that in nature there were hints of God available for any thinking person; all you had to do was to stand beneath the starry wonder of the sky, or kneel in the still, numinous hush of a forest glade. (No wonder we used to trundle our youth groups out into the countryside figuring they might bump into God!) Of course, if nature did not grab you, you could turn to the inner world, tracing patterns of amazing grace within your own memory, for surely religious experience also reflected the mystery of God. But with the rise of science and psychology, the whole idea of a general revelation crashed. Scientists came along and relabeled the natural world without recourse to God-talk. And then, as the century unfolded, Dr. Freud showed up to explain pathologies where once we had found God's presence. All of a sudden we were left with nothing more than special revelation, namely Scripture, tradition, and some shaky verses from our favorite hymns.

So what did we do? In the twentieth century, we backed off, and redesigned our ideas of revelation. With nature emptied and the self uncertain, we began talking of God revealed in the events of history. We wrote big books about "the mighty acts of God."[4] Like the psalmist, we recited God-events in sequence: Abraham trekking to an unknown land, Moses leading a gaggle of slaves up out of Egypt, tablets of law tossed from Mt. Sinai, then sad Jeremiah trudging off with the exiles. We assembled the mighty acts of God in sequence, one after another, into a grand story of God and humanity. No wonder we were so eager to embrace the whole idea of narrative preaching. We told God as a story, our story that ultimately led us to Jesus Christ and the community we call church. What was revelation? Why, nothing less than the Bible, "the book of the acts of God." No wonder generations of seminary students have giggled, singing, "The B-I-B-L-E, that's the book for me." There you are: objective biblical events, "the B-I-B-L-E," and once again, please note, a personal pronoun, "me." General revelation has virtually disappeared. At the same time, the story of God with us, "our story," seems to have separated from the rest of human history.

Now then, we tinkered with the doctrine of revelation in still another way. We dumped the whole idea of dogmatic truth. God's revelation does not disclose truths, principles, teachings, or dogma. No, God's revelation is personal, God is self-revealed in the person of Jesus. Oddly enough, we skipped the teachings of Jesus, because at the turn of the century Albert Schweitzer told us they were an "interim ethic," thus nothing more than short-lived apocalyptic fluff.[5] No, we said, the person of Jesus is the revealing of God—even though we actually knew very little about a personal Jesus. In so doing, we ended up with a high but somewhat unintelligible Christology. Nonetheless, we urged our congregations to have a personal relationship with Jesus so they could be saved inside of themselves, personally! And, in our pulpits, salvation got taken over by what Philip Rieff once termed "the triumph of the therapeutic."[6] Underlying the New Homiletic was a sense of biblical story, and a concern for individual personal experience.

Then, all of a sudden, in 1970, the same year Fred Craddock penned his brilliant *As One without Authority*, and Henry Mitchell published *the* volume on *Black Preaching*, unexpectedly, biblical scholar Brevard Childs wrote a book announcing the impending collapse of the Biblical Theology movement.[7] Oh, perhaps, it was not quite dead, for it is still sputtering in Yale's "postliberal theology," but it was significantly wounded. Then, in 1997, Brevard Childs wrote another essay, even more poignant, saying that for one brief, bright moment God had shone on America in the theology of Karl Barth, but now it was over, dead, destroyed by scholars who refused to believe in the authority of Scripture.[8] Can we admit the New Homiletic faded because it rested on an insupportable split between objective biblical revelation and individual experience—a split that was built into the Protestant era from the start?

Interpersonal Consciousness and the Interhuman

So here we are now in a somewhat bleak twenty-first century, and here's a question: People say we are postmodern. What is postmodern all about? How has our world changed?

Take a look at the arts. Back in the eighteenth century, artists would set up their easels and paint what they saw. They saw perspective, and they painted what was in front of them. They produced art we all understood. But in the nineteenth century Impressionists came along and painted what they saw, but in action, and with a dash of feeling stirred in with the paint. Nowadays artists are going even further. They are painting what they see as it appears on the screen of consciousness along with associations, memories, fantasies, feelings, sexual promptings, cultural archetypes, and anything else that shows up. Artists are not trying to annoy us. No, they are doing what artists are supposed to do, namely, show us reality.

The same sort of thing happened in literature. When William Thackeray wrote *Vanity Fair* halfway through the nineteenth century, he told a story of Becky Sharpe chronologically, start to finish, and always from a fixed, third-person, objective viewpoint.[9] But ever since William Faulkner, novels have been quite different. There may be many voices involved in telling a story, from different times and places, with different styles and points of view. There has been a shift toward consciousness. For example, a few years ago a short-story writer attempted to bend syntax by describing many things happening simultaneously in human consciousness. A man is with friends at a small party. He glances at a woman across the room and in a flashback recalls a sexual evening they had together, at the same time he hears footsteps climbing stairs to an adjoining apartment, and he reaches for food remembering the same smells and tastes from childhood, all the while worrying over his failing financial condition.[10] Notice these many things were filling consciousness all at same time. Why mention writers? Because, good writers also are trying to show us reality.

Now let's see what is going on when we gather in a room while someone speaks. We could study the event objectively, hiring photographers to snap pictures from all angles. We could tape record everything spoken, as well as questions afterward. We could go further, asking everyone's name, address, age, sex, marital status, and church denomination. Still more, we could test blood pressures and pulse rates, before and after. We could even design an exit poll. Nothing but the facts, please! But notice what's being left out, namely interpersonal consciousness. Reality has to include our merged inner worlds filled with memories, images from TV screens, dear faces of the living and the dead, recent sex, the burdened awareness of a bad war dragging on, and maybe worry over too many foreclosures in a crumbling economy. Think of all that is actually happening in the reality of a moment, in the here and now. Walker Percy tells the story of a man who learned everything he could learn about the world—biology, chemistry, physics, medicine, geography, you name it, he learned it—finally, he seemed to know everything that could be known, but admitted sadly, "I myself was left over!"[11] Our reality, to be real, must include interpersonal realms of consciousness.

Now, if an understanding of the world "out there" has changed, what about the personal pronoun "I"? Remember Descartes said "I," and so did Luther. Oh, it is not merely that there are many viewpoints on any subject these days. There are, and we should have them in mind whenever we speak. But lately, philosophers are mentioning something else, something they call the "interhuman." Who do you read? You read Austrian sociologist Alfred Schütz, French ethicist Emanuel Lévinas, old Jewish scholar Martin Buber, and maybe theologians Edward Farley and Paul Sponheim.[12] They are bypassing the subject-object split by recognizing a reality that undergirds both, a web of relationship they call the interhuman. Are we ever individual? No, from conception until we leave the womb, we are in relationship. Thereafter, we are never out of relationship, for even when we are alone, our nature has been shaped by interrelating; others are ever with us in consciousness. Tony Kushner, our finest contemporary playwright, says it bluntly: "The smallest divisible human unit is two people; not one. One is a fiction."[13] The New Homiletic focused on the individual, a single self in self-awareness with personal needs. After all, we wanted to be relevant. But, if "one is a fiction," did we end up with a kind of unreality? Somehow we must learn to address the interhuman, which incidentally is closer to what Jesus called the "kingdom of God" than the fiction of an individual self.

Tinkering with the New Homiletic

All right, time now to talk about preaching. We are living in a brave, somewhat inchoate new age, what homiletic must we have? How must preaching change? Let's begin with some small-scale, minor-key tinkering.

Here's a start: somehow we must recover theology. Back at the beginning of the twentieth century, P. T. Forsythe in his Yale Lectures on

Preaching pleaded for a return to the Bible.[14] As historians have mentioned, Forsythe sounded like a Barth before Barth. Well, we listened, for there are scarcely any sermons these days that do not begin with a biblical passage, often, if compulsively, from the lectionary. Certainly, the New Homiletic pushed the issue, for with few exceptions, we wrote about how to preach the Bible. Sometimes there was even a snide repudiation of topical preaching, including theological topics. Systematic theology, like rhetoric, was considered suspiciously Greek and therefore unbiblical in character.

What has been the result of this emphasis? According to some studies, in spite of our biblical preaching, people do not know the Bible any better than they did in the 1940s, but tragically they do not know theology at all. A hundred years ago, scratch a Presbyterian and you were bound to get an amateur theologian. Nowadays, scratch a Presbyterian and all you will get is a Republican. Laugh, but do not laugh loudly. If theology is gone, then people have nothing left with which to interpret life but their own social commitments. They are Republicans, or Masons, or black, or gay, or Democrats, southern or northern, hawks or pacifists, or just flag-waving All-Americans. What's more, they interpret the Bible from these same social commitments. Maybe we will have to stop handing out therapies and teach our congregations how to think theologically all over again. Somehow our preaching must help to restore a theological awareness to the American mind.

Now while we are at it, here's another Greek idea. Homiletics used to be called "sacred rhetoric." Oh, we're not going to rehearse the classics, trace our way back through Quintilian to Cicero to Aristotle. We could do worse, but there have been twenty centuries of rhetoric since the Greeks and Romans; we can study contemporary rhetoricians. A good rhetorician can tell you how to form words so as to convey meaning to twenty-first-century people. In the New Homiletic, we were busy trying to reach beyond conventional pulpit practice and find new ways to preach the gospel, but we did not trust rhetoric. Like theology, rhetoric smelled Greek rather than biblical, or if it was not Greek, then it was manipulation or "spin."

No, we need rhetoric, because speaking to congregations is entirely different from one-to-one conversations. And different from visual aids as well. Instead of preaching, do not start showing films. After Marshall McLuhan many people figured, the more media the better.[15] But then a smart student of McLuhan's, Walter Ong, came along and proved different media do different things. If you want to form faith, for heaven's sake speak, because words get close to human understanding, and what's more, words unify. Films will drive images into individual subjectivity, but oddly enough the visual does not unify.[16] So maybe the Bible has it right with its strange confidence in words. Rhetoric shares the same confidence. We must do our homework and recover the task of learning sacred rhetoric. What's more, we must research a new rhetoric to address the interhuman, quite beyond American individualism.

Here's a third try at tinkering (see, three points, but no poem!): we've got to recover the prophetic. I have spent most of my life with seminary students. I love them all, and seldom ever talk about them. But here is an observation: nowadays students seem more frightened than ever before, and particularly frightened about preaching. Why? Probably because they have learned from us. Let me be blunt. When America launched a preemptive war, a wicked war according to any reading of Christian "Just War" tradition, local pulpits pretty much said nothing. And when America wrote policy, overriding Geneva Conventions, to justify torture, which we then proceeded to practice, again local pulpits said almost nothing. What was the matter with us? Were we unable to break out of the Bible? Or had we decided Christian faith was basically personal therapy? Or were our congregations too Republican to risk comment? Agreed, ministers are having a tough time these days—did I read that nationally, a thousand clergy a week are being eased out of their pulpits? In a divided land, packed with social stridency, it is risky to speak on any subject. But look, we cannot drop prophecy from Scripture, or the prophetic from our pulpits. We cannot echo Billy Graham, who when criticized for his silence in the midst of civil rights struggles, replied testily that he was "a gospeller, not an Old Testament prophet." No, the gospel has prophetic dimension because Jesus' message of the kingdom of God is intrinsically prophetic. So much for a little tinkering with homiletic practice.

Finding Our Calling

Time now to step beyond tinkering. In every age, preaching must find a special calling. What must preaching become in the twenty-first century? What is our calling?

Let's go back and begin with a peculiar fact: René Descarte was a child of the church, who believed in God. Nevertheless, as a philosopher, he knew he had to begin his search for truth by doubting all inherited certainties. Finally, he hit on his one sure thing: "I think, therefore I am." His "I am," while not exactly blurted from a burning bush, was significant, for without even trying, he reshaped both faith and reason. If Descartes was an objective observer who looked out at the world rationally, his God turned out to be exactly the same thing. God was a transcendent God, overseeing the world with divine reason. So there was a kind of profound correspondence between humanity and God. We were reasoning people shaped in the image of an unseen but rational God, a God like us—so, ultimately, the universe was friendly. What happened during the twentieth century was that the sweet sense of correspondence between God and humanity shattered, and our human world became strangely bereft.

Back in the nineteenth century, Robert Browning wrote of a young woman who woke everyday in sunshine singing, "Mornings at seven, the hillsides dew-pearled; God's in his heaven, all's right with the world."[17] A cheerful sense of correspondence! But a hundred years later, the priest in a Tennessee Williams play said it differently. Listen, as the Reverend Shannon tells of a Sunday morning:

> I had prepared a sermon—meek, apologetic—I threw it away, tossed it into the chancel. Look here, I said, I shouted. I'm tired of conducting services in praise and worship of a *senile delinquent*, yeah that's what I said, I shouted . . . All your western theologies . . . are based on the concept of God as a senile delinquent. "Go home," the Reverend Shannon shouted, "Go home and close . . . your windows and doors against the truth about God![18]

Clearly, for the Reverend Shannon, a comforting sense of correspondence was no longer available. He was, of course, kicked out of his church.

So here's the problem: if heaven has been erased and "Our Father" has faded in whispers of disbelief, then human beings become brutishly human, we lose the *imago Dei*. So how can we reinstate a notion of correspondence, faith in a living God, and humanity shaped in God's image? There is the job description. And why is it our job? Why, because the apostle Paul said, "Faith comes from hearing." How can we preach so as to reach the careless mind of our age, careless and copeless, yet longing for something more than a better sex life and an IRA? How can we preach so, gradually, a sense of correspondence may be fabricated all over again? "Faith," said Paul, "Faith comes from hearing."

Here's *Step One*: once more preaching must convey a sense of present mystery. In a lost, overanalyzed society, can we recover primal mystery? Our glib age, crowded with too much information, has no patience with the unknowable. And often our pulpits have been as glib, eager to dish up answers, but unwilling to invoke mystery. But there's the job: "preaching as invocation." If all our sermons can do is to declare a past-tense God revealed in stories scribbled in an ancient Bible-book, we are in trouble. Not much mystery if you can point to God, G-o-d, on the page of a book. In Tony Kushner's astonishing play *Angels in America*, when the angels do show up they turn out to be a trio of old men lugging around a huge book, claiming that in the absence of God, they cannot say anything unless it is authorized by the book.[19] Probably our pulpits inspired the scene. Have we forgotten the way Jesus spoke? His words were filled with a huge sense of the impending future of God. He painted pictures of the promises of God coming true and invited people to step right into God's future, and live as a new humanity in the *basileia* of God! Look, God is working to fulfill future promises now, so *basileia*, "kingdom," is a "happening" in which, know it or not, we are living right now. Presence is impossible if all we can preach is a past-tense God. You cannot invoke past-tense presence; it does not work. No, to have presence, there must be a future we can talk about, anticipate, and gleefully await. Presence is something that overarches our lives, past to future, future to past. Special revelation will always turn glib, if all it can do is promote *us*—our book, our story, our church. Mystery happens when we stumble on something we do not have and cannot explain, something that drops us to our knees stammering. What preaching needs nowadays is more stammering—awe instead of answers, even answers from the Bible. Once more, preaching must be invocation, the invocation of God's mysterious Presence.

Now, *Step Two*: somehow we must strive to reinstate general revelation. People have no real interest in opening a Bible or coming to church unless they have some minimal awareness of unnamed presence impinging on their lives. So we must show folk signs of the presence of God beyond the Bible page, not pointing to where God once was, but where God will be and is now! It is tough to talk of general revelation when most people these days are alienated from nature. The "heavens may declare the glory of God," but city lights can dim the stars. As for farm animals, these days most of us meet them saran-wrapped on meat-market counters. And how can we turn inward nowadays and expect to find God amid all the psychobabble? Not easily. So until we are able to feel kinship with nature or somehow rediscover the mystery of our own being, temporarily we better search for signs of God elsewhere. These days, at least until NASA flings too much hardware into space, there still may be a kind of astonishment at mysteries of the cosmos, astonishment at us little people blundering about on a spin-ball earth out among the flickering stars. And maybe we can learn to speak of an equally mysterious space, namely space in between ourselves and others, interhuman space. In the past, we have tried to document God's presence by telling stories of individuals who have lived their pieties impressively—incidently, almost all of them were men! In an age when music is made by groups, and films feature people in their togetherness, can we learn to find presence in interactive humanity, living toward the future of God.

Now, here's a crucial follow-up: How do we know where God may be found? To answer, you do not have to tear out a Bible page to fling at your congregation. No, you argue from the future of God backward to now. Listen to Jesus speaking of kingdom-come in the Beatitudes. In God's new social order the hungry will be fed, yes, and the poor will be raised up, yes, and the powerless empowered. And those who grieve for the way of the world will find their delight. Peacemakers will triumph, and those who are persecuted will celebrate. So whenever and wherever you see beatitudes beginning to come true, there is where you will find the presence of an unseen, astonishingly modest God.

So let us go and speak words that God will set on our lips. Let us invoke the present-tense mystery of God, a God we cannot fully understand even if we were to memorize the entire Bible. In every new age, God appears incognito in different garb, but always God is mysterious, for mystery is the nature of God-with-us. You know, these days the evangelicalist movement seems to trouble us mainline types, but at least evangelicalists are trying to do what we have failed to do, namely, to reach out with

Christian faith where faith has been forgotten or is as yet undiscovered. They may do it badly, pushing impossible fundamentalism and building megachurches, as well as selling their souls to calculating politicians, but at least they are trying—there is something evangelical in the evangelicalist movement. Mainline Protestant Christianity has not reached out across economic lines, or racial lines, or ethnic lines—and good heavens, listen to us on the subject of immigration. No, we have sought our own kind, thank you, in smug disobedience before God. Like an executive sales staff, we have promoted our churches, as if churches ever saved anyone! How can we break out of ourselves? Maybe we cannot. And if we cannot, surely God will shatter and remake us. But meanwhile what we can do is to lean far, far out from our pulpits to declare a God who goes beyond the biblical page, and beyond our churches as well, a strange, alien God whose holiness is always hidden by our blindness.

Listen, in the new century, God is a Consciousness, capital C, Conscious of us, a mysterious cosmic Consciousness in whom we live and move and have our being. When you stand in the pulpit, speak to your people of this mysterious Consciousness of God. There is a woodcut of a preacher in an old-fashioned high pulpit. The picture shows him leaning way out toward his people as he speaks. Behind him there is a swirl of mysterious dark, somehow like a Presence. Dear friends, the picture is you. You preach in the mystery of Presence, a presence of God you must invoke with every word you speak.

Meanwhile, if you have not done so, go read the New Homiletic. After all, the New Homiletic was sort of a baby step in the right direction.

Responses

Pablo A. Jiménez

It is rather difficult to write a response to an essay written by an author of whom you are in awe. Buttrick's contribution to the New Homiletic has been enormous, placing him in a unique position to reflect on its past, present, and future.

In his essay, Buttrick correctly affirms that the New Homiletic stands between two epochs: modernity and postmodernity. Philosophers use the adjective *liminal* to describe phenomena that stand at the threshold of a new era. "Liminal" describes something that is transitional; something placed in between two states, phases, or conditions.

Buttrick affirms that the New Homiletic is a product of modernity. For him, it is "literature on the cusp, scribbled at the weary end of an age . . . the New Homiletic was the product of a particular waning age but, at best, was trying to tiptoe toward an emerging future." And this is where I part ways with Buttrick, for I see the New Homiletic as a rupture with modernity.

Jean-François Lyotard, the French sociologist, defines postmodernity as an attitude of incredulity toward the master narratives or narrative archetypes that sustained the modern world.[20] These master narratives legitimized the crimes of modernity, crimes such as the violent conquest of America, the genocide against indigenous peoples, slavery, the oppression of women, and racism, among many others. Such crimes ultimately decried the basic tenets of modernity. The rationalistic view of life, with its blind faith on progress, did not lead us to a better world. No, it led us to Auschwitz; it led us to a nuclear standoff; it led us to a polluted and decaying world. For these reasons, Lyotard affirms that Auschwitz is "the crime that opens postmodernity."[21]

Departing from this definition, we can affirm that the New Homiletic is thoroughly postmodern. Let us take, as an example, Fred B. Craddock's *As One without Authority*. In this seminal book, Craddock defies the homiletic model that dominated the English-speaking world for centuries: the British epistemological or rationalistic style. Influenced by classical rhetoric, it presented the Christian message as propositional truth based on a deductive outline. This is the preaching methodology exemplified by Spurgeon's sermons and by Broadus's writings.

The New Homiletic revolted against the traditional sermon for the same reasons postmodern thought revolted against modernity. The traditional sermon, with its rigid logic, was a tool used to legitimize Christendom's blind faith on modernity's promise.

This leads us to a second trait of postmodernity: the affirmation of the "micro-narratives," or specific stories of minority groups and foreign cultures.[22] Once again, the New Homiletic showed its postmodern penchant in books such as Henry H. Mitchell's *Black Preaching*. These writings, which analyze homiletics from the perspective of peoples previously relegated to history's basement, are not narcissistic interpretations of individual social commitments. They are theological treatises that affirm God's acceptance of and presence in communities despised and oppressed by modernity. They celebrate the presence of God's Word, which also dwells among communities previously victimized by modernity.

I remember my first encounter with the New Homiletic, mediated by the writings of Ronald J. Allen. The experience was liberating. The teachings I found in these books allowed me to transcend the rigid homiletic models that colonial Christianity had taught the church in the Spanish-speaking Caribbean. All of a sudden, I was not bound anymore by a homiletic that stressed individual salvation, read the Bible in an ahistorical way, and spiritualized poverty and disease. I found a homiletic that took seriously my social location, allowing me to preach as the bilingual and bicultural man that I am.

Nonetheless, we cannot disregard the perils that postmodern thought presents for both society and the church. The fragmentation of truth, the attitude of incredulity, the mass market of ideas, the openness to non-Christian spirituality, the simulacra and simulation produced by the media, and the proliferation of nonplaces are but a few of its dangers.[23] Moreover, Justo L. González tackles Lyotard's definition, asserting that postmodernity has created "a new metanarrative. And, paradoxically enough, this new metanarrative is that there are no metanarratives. . . . In such a world, no new metanarratives will have the power to change the *status quo*, and thus the structures of power which developed under modern metanarrative will remain."[24]

González's critique gives us ammo to analyze, question, and even challenge postmodernity's attitude toward Christendom, in specific, and Christianity, in general. It also gives us footing to call for the recovery of Christian theology and the recovery of the prophetic aspects of preaching, called for by Buttrick in his essay. Postmodern thought cannot silence the church.

Buttrick ends his essay suggesting two steps for recuperating the *imago Dei* lost due to postmodern chatter. The first step is preaching that conveys a sense of present mystery and the second one is preaching that somehow reinstates general revelation. I welcome and applaud these suggestions. I think that Protestant God-talk sometimes borders in heresy. Fundamentalist preaching proclaims a God who has already said all there is to say through Scripture, exalting the inerrancy of the Bible. Neo-Pentecostal preaching proclaims a God bound by promises to bless and prosper those believers who claim material wealth and spiritual salvation. And mainline Protestant preaching has perfected the sermon that barely mentions God, stressing either the psychological dimensions of pastoral care or the social responsibility of the church. These emphases foster concepts of God that lack a sense of mystery and that somehow restrict revelation to the written page or the Christian community.

Of course, Buttrick's language differs from my preferred ways of expressing the faith. I chose to reread his call to "convey a sense of present mystery" as a call to stress God's "otherness" and freedom. "Otherness" not only affirms God's mysterious nature, but also allows the preacher to take into consideration the social locations of the audience. This is of particular importance for racial-ethnic preachers whose communities had been labeled as "other" by modernity. Once again, a homiletic that takes into consideration God's "otherness" leads oppressed communities to the liberation and freedom promised by the gospel of Jesus Christ to all.

By the same token, I chose to read Buttrick's call to "reinstate general revelation" as another idea amenable to a homiletic of liberation. General revelation affirms God's self-disclosure and communication in the universe and in the created world.[25] If this is true, then it is possible to find manifestations of God's grace and love in Latino culture, in particular, and in every tribe and nation.

Alyce M. McKenzie

David Buttrick's original proposal in *Homiletic: Moves and Structures* used the philosophical school of phenomenology to convey that there are certain common dynamics to the ways human beings experience life and form faith. *Homiletic* was filled with descriptions of how faith forms in consciousness, not just of individuals, but also of communities. Buttrick recommended replacing the static outline form of preaching with what he called "moves," a series of "rhetorical units" or "language modules" put together by some sort of logic. He believed that moves formed in consciousness to pattern understanding.[26]

Homiletic included specific sermonic strategies for opening, developing, and closing moves to shape faith and transform identity. His book was immensely helpful. The very prescriptions that garnered criticism for being modernist overgeneralizations from a specific philosophical school proved strategically savvy in the teaching and formation of sermons.

In this essay Buttrick doesn't offer a description, critique, or defense of his own work and a prescription explicitly based on it for the future of preaching. That's what I expected. Instead, in the first part of the paper he holds a mirror up to the New Homiletic and asks it if it likes what it sees. In the second part he suggests some transformations that are not mere surface improvements, but must come from within.

Rather than respond to the paper I was expecting him to write, I'll respond to the one he did write. I'm going to comment, first, on why contemporary preachers should care about what happens when the New Homiletic looks in Buttrick's mirror. Then I'm going to say Amen to a couple of the transformations he suggests, and explain the reasons for my enthusiasm.

Buttrick says the New Homiletic faded because it was based on a false split between biblical story and personal experience. In other words, he is saying that it faded because it was based on modernist assumptions. Says Buttrick, "The New Homiletic focused on the individual, a single self in self-awareness with personal needs."

I found this mirror image quite interesting. I've always thought that the New Homiletic thought of itself as postmodern before postmodern was the thing to be. It prided itself on turning away from the premodernist preoccupation with the presentation of objective truths and turning toward the experience of listening and the needs of listeners. But maybe Buttrick is right, and the New Homiletic was based on the assumption of universality in how we experience and process life events. Maybe Buttrick's paper rightly exposes the modernist assumptions that caused the New Homiletic to fade. It assumes a universality about how we experience and process life events. In some cases this process was described as induction (Craddock), in some as a narrative plot (Rice, Lowry), and in some as the phenomeno-logical formation of faith in consciousness (Buttrick).

Buttrick holds the mirror up to contemporary art and literature as well as homiletics. He shows us the turn toward the viewer using the example of Impressionism in art. He shows us the turn toward the reader in twentieth-century literature, using the example of novels in the latter half of the twen-tieth century, with their eschewal of the third-person objective narrator in favor of shifting, more limited viewpoints.

The paper is not liberally sprinkled with the word *consciousness*. But reading between the lines, I think Buttrick stands by the usefulness of the concept of consciousness that he highlighted in his original proposal in *Homiletic*. As homiletics moves further into the twenty-first century, But-trick points out that we can't go back to the split between objective and subjective. The features of the world out there and our perception of them are inextricably intertwined. That seems to be his definition of postmod-ernism. Given that intertwined phenomenon, consciousness is still the con-cept that Buttrick favors to express the reality that undergirds both object and subject. In this paper at least, he favors describing it in terms of a term favored by philosophers, theologians, ethicists, and sociologists: *the realm of the interhuman*.

What do the New Homiletic and beyond it, preaching in general these days, see when they gaze into Buttrick's mirror? The New Homi-letic preached the text; we need to make sure we preach the gospel. The New Homiletic tended to mirror the individualism it supposedly reacted against. We need to preach to the interhuman realm, not the "fiction of the individualized self." Preaching can fall into the trap of giving answers. We need to respect the mystery. Preaching can tend to limit God to the pages of the biblical text, narrowing special revelation to bibliolatry. By contrast, preaching needs to alert listeners to God at work beyond the Bible in the realms of nature, human relationships, and communities. Preaching can tend to have a past reference. It needs instead to invoke visions of what the future holds for us when we receive and live by the good news.

Buttrick's prescriptions for preaching in the twenty-first century grow out of his critique of the New Homiletic and of preaching in general at the present moment. These prescriptions come through in three "tinker-ing" suggestions followed by two of what Buttrick considers to be more

substantive recommendations for our vocation of preaching. I find Buttrick's three "tinkering" suggestions to be far more than merely surficial.
They are that we recover the theological, rhetorical, and prophetic functions of preaching today. Buttrick focuses largely on the theological and
the prophetic. I wish he had elaborated on the second (rhetorical) recovery
plan. My own recent work has focused on recovering the teaching function
of preaching through the use of story, imagery, and metaphor. Given his
advice on imaging concepts in *Homiletic*, I was eager to hear his current
views on how preachers can use rhetorical forms to capture the imagination
and fulfill the theological and prophetic functions of a sermon.

His point about recovering the theological function of preaching
deserves a hearty chorus of Amens! Says Buttrick, "If theology is gone, then
people have nothing left with which to interpret life but their own social
commitments." He expresses concern that people today not only don't
know their Bibles any better than they did in the 1940s, but also suffer
from theological ignorance. The assumption of the New Homiletic of the
1970s and '80s, that people knew their Bibles well enough to contextualize
an aesthetically inviting, inductive sermon, is not the case in 2009. With
biblical illiteracy and theological hunger in place, Buttrick's proposal that
we reinstate the theological function of preaching is far more urgent than a
suggestion for tinkering.

So is his insistence that we reinstate the prophetic function of preaching. His charge that we have been preaching the Bible but not the gospel, in part due to the New Homiletic's disdain for theological and topical
preaching, hits the mark. So does his challenge that a whole generation
of preachers is confusing the Christian faith with personal therapy or, as
some have said, with "hospice preaching" (keep them comfortable until
they die). Buttrick's word of challenge, again, is much more profound than
mere tinkering.

After Buttrick offers his suggestions on tinkering, he moves on to ask,
"What is our calling as preachers in the twenty-first century?" His answer is
twofold. One is that preaching needs to "convey a sense of present mystery."
The second is that preaching "must strive to reinstate general revelation."
In other words, it must "show folk signs of the presence of God beyond
the Bible page." Buttrick's recommendations here are invaluable for contemporary preaching. He suggests that we "argue from the future of God

backward to now." "Whenever and wherever you see beatitudes beginning to come true, there is where you will find the presence of an unseen, astonishingly modest God."

The critique of Buttrick's approach was that it overgeneralized from one philosophical school and one practitioner's perspective. Perhaps what the New Homiletic learns when it looks in the mirror is that the mirror needs to be bigger. We need to see lots of faces and hear lots of voices. Buttrick's work continues to be an invaluable resource in my own teaching whenever I try to help a student discern the difference between a static outline and a sequence of moves that might actually gain and sustain interest, touch emotions, teach the mind, and transform identity.

His contribution continues to invite the participation of others, who learn from it and put it into practice even as they take issue with it.

Mobile, Episodic, Intentional

Richard L. Eslinger

M y motivation for attempting a book on recent homiletic method in the mid-1980s was, first, to map the changing homiletical terrain for myself. Having been trained in the "old school" of sermonic outlines, points, and illustrations to "ram it home," I was by then certain that something profound was occurring, a vast sea change within the waters of preaching. Thus, my first book—besides a collection of sermons written earlier—was born: *A New Hearing: Living Options in Homiletic Method.*[1] The five homileticians/preachers I discuss in that book—this volume's "Venerables," Charles Rice, Fred Craddock, Henry Mitchell, Eugene Lowry, and David Buttrick—had graciously provided me with oral and written materials as I worked on it; they also graced me with sermons illustrative of their methods. I now count these five colleagues as friends—after all, they have been mentors and family for over thirty years!

Twenty years later, I was honored to attend a remarkable conference at Lexington Theological Seminary where my colleague, Wes Allen, assembled the five "Venerables" who were the subjects of my explorations in *A New Hearing*. At "The Re(New)ed Homiletic" event Allen achieved a homiletical first in gathering together the "New Hearing Five" for that conference and now for this book.[2] That the future of our discipline is in good hands is evidenced by Allen's introductory essay on these "pillars" of the New Homiletic (which should be required reading in every introduction to preaching class), as well as by the diverse group of smart and insightful colleagues in the homiletics guild whom he has assembled as respondents to each of the Venerables. I rejoice in the wealth of their assessments and constructive offerings.

I have shaped this epilogue as a bookend to that fine introduction, which I commend whole cloth with hardly any even minor quibbles. Indeed, I offer these remarks primarily by way of some elaboration and expansion. Of course, my comments are contained within three points!

The Roots of the New Homiletic

Numerous contributors to the project have noted that the New Homiletic, as any movement of reform, had its ideological roots in a variety of precursors. It did not simply pop into existence in 1970 *ex nihilo*! Dale Andrews is especially helpful in charting the work of those who "broke through dominant propositional and deductive forms of preaching in Western mainline church traditions . . ."[3] Being the multidisciplinary field that it is, the roots of the New Homiletic also drew on a wide range of emerging movements beyond specifically homiletical boundaries. A short listing of these rootages would need to include the following:

1. *The Resurgence of Biblical Narrative.* Those dominant forms of preaching in Western mainline churches would not have been broken without the pioneering work of biblical scholars and literary critics who rediscovered the narrativity of Scripture for the Western church. (I say "rediscover" for two reasons. On one hand,

there had been an "eclipse" of biblical narrative since the Enlightenment[4] while, on the other hand, within the African American church, the narrative quality of the Bible had never been lost![5]) With this resurgence of biblical narrative came a companion reform in the dominant models of interpretation. The long-reigning "hermeneutics of distillation" was finally giving way to other less rationalistic approaches to the text. Once Amos Wilder identified the parables of Jesus as narrative metaphors,[6] the "main idea" hermeneutic of Adolf Jülicher[7] was toppled from its dominance (although on any given Sunday you can hear Jülicher's disciples still questing after some parable's main idea!).

2. *Paradigm Shift in the Vernacular.* While several of our Venerables and their commentators have noted the influence of Heidegger, Bultmann, and the leaders of the New Hermeneutic upon the sea change in homiletics, David Buttrick has been central in his enduring analysis of the communal vernacular of the culture. He noted in *Homiletic* that ours is a culture of "rapidly changing language."[8] More recently, he put it this way: "The world is in the process of changing its mind."[9] These profound changes, along with the emergence of various post-Enlightenment hermeneutics, conspired to make any homiletic grounded in discursive rhetoric impossible to sustain.

3. *Liturgical Reforms of the Second Vatican Council.* The reforms of Vatican II provided an essential foundation for the later reforms that we now speak of as the New Homiletic. The sequence of first a process of liturgical renewal and then of homiletical reform makes absolute sense. In fact, it is difficult to imagine the sequence occurring in reverse. And in spite of comments from some within the New Homiletic Five, the advent of the Roman Catholic Lectionary remains one of the most unexpected and powerful influences on the recovery of biblical preaching in the twentieth century. (Who would have imagined this reform being a gift of Rome to the Protestant church?) Among the five Venerables, Charles Rice has been the most forceful in his insistence on the liturgical and sacramental context of the sermon.[10] Preaching is a liturgical act, of course.

4. *The Civil Rights Movement.* For many majority-culture Christians, the first significant encounter with African American preaching occurred during the civil rights struggles of the 1950s and '60s. A number of us returned from these profound and moving experiences to our pastorates or to seminary never to be the same. Among the myriad of memories to be sorted out were worship services of fervent prayer and praise and preaching at once prophetic and pastoral and celebratory. As Dale Andrews comments in his essay, "the 'new hearing' movement of homiletics mirrors black preaching traditions."[11] Henry Mitchell then provided an in-depth analysis of the experiences that remain powerful and formative influences. For these events of African American preaching and worship and for Mitchell's interpretive brilliance, we are deeply grateful.[12]

Commonalities and Characteristics

When Wes Allen turns to the task of offering a sketch of the New Homiletic's characteristics, he notes that his listing includes several "common denominators . . . meant to be illustrative more than exhaustive."[13] Rather than expanding upon Allen's three qualities, I see the opportunity at this place of summary and reflection to glean additional insights from our five Venerables and from our savvy commentators. I may add some reflections as well.

The first characteristic pertaining to the New Homiletic, Allen offers, is that of the turn to the hearer. Rather than the primary interest of the preacher being that of constructing a persuasive argument, the New Homiletic "focused instead on how people in the pew listen, how they experience language." He adds, sounding very much like how Fred Craddock would put it, that "this approach assumes the hearer is a partner in the sermonic event."[14] Just here, however, a number of commentators have criticized the New Homiletic for its undue individualism. The turn is to *the* hearer (in the singular)! Indeed, David Buttrick is blunt in his critique of his colleagues at this point: "The New Homiletic focused on the individual, a single self in self-awareness with personal needs. After all, we wanted to be relevant. But, if 'one is a fiction,' did we end up with a kind of unreality?"[15] As with some other judgments of my beloved mentor, a comment (addressed to me) by my dean at Boston University School of Theology might be in order: "The broom is not an instrument of precision!" First, a community of homileticians cannot shift their hermeneutic to that of some narrative perspective while remaining caught in the fiction of "the one." Any narrative theology worth its salt necessarily involves a community shaped by the ongoing recital of its core narratives.[16] Second, as Alyce McKenzie muses, Buttrick may be on target in assuming some sort of universality to human experience—thereby privileging some sort of normative social and theological perspective. But the postmodern stance of the New Homiletic seemed to pride itself "on turning away from the premodernist preoccupation with the presentation of objective truths . . ."[17] Does not the New Homiletic represent a stance that incorporates both individual and communal considerations? Certainly for Henry Mitchell, Buttrick's judgment cannot be sustained. Henry Mitchell and his colleague African American homileticians consistently speak of the dual consciousness of the hearers— the sermon addresses embodied persons at a soul depth and the entire assembly as well. There is an "interactive human consciousness" addressed by the preacher, both personal and communal, never an either/or.[18] David Buttrick speaks of this "world" of the hearers as the "interhuman."[19] At this point can we say that most of us working within some New Homiletic vineyard or other (1) are still likely to be contaminated with shreds and shards of modernity at times, but (2) are deeply committed to Pablo Jiménez's "rupture with modernity"?[20]

Allen's next characteristic proposed as typifying the New Homiletic is that of a paradigm shift in sermonic form. Sermons "move us," Allen adds.[21] In my introduction to preaching class, I repeatedly scribble on the whiteboard or smartboard the following mantra: "Mobile, Episodic, Intentional." These three qualities obtain for much of Scripture, especially biblical narrative; they should be, too, the marks of good preaching. That the New Homiletic insisted on a refreshing sermonic mobility is evident to anyone who has read the work of our Venerable Five. Eugene Lowry perhaps says it best when he distinguishes between "doing time in the pulpit" and "doing space."[22] Lowry's helpful chart sets forth the alternatives: a construction model of building ideas versus a narrative shaping of the homiletical plot.[23] David Buttrick insured that students of his homiletic could not even speak of "the Buttrick method" without invoking mobility.

For Buttrick, each unit of conceptual and imagistic language within any homiletical plot is a "move." But each move also invokes a strong sense of the episodic quality of this renewed preaching. "David Buttrick's work has been episodal all along," notes Eugene Lowry.[24] And Lowry's response to Allen's invitation to "name or nuance" a core contribution for the future surprisingly led to a much more emphatic development of the episodal.[25] Finally, my introduction to preaching slogan concludes with "Intentional." Buttrick underlined this performative dimension of Scripture when he announced that he was more interested in what a text wants to do than in what it means. Consequently, many of us in the homiletics guild will respond to a student's early offering in preaching lab by (nicely) asking, "So what?" Henry Mitchell expands on this performative intention of the biblical text and the biblical sermon by speaking of the latter's "behavioral purpose." Beyond all other goals and objectives of any sermon, Mitchell insists, "the bottom line is behavioral." He adds, "Every preacher needs to choose an appropriate behavioral purpose, as opposed to a cognitive purpose such as facts or truth, as a final goal."[26] Mobile, episodic, intentional—these are the qualities of sermons reflective of this renewed hearing.

The third paradigm shift Allen notes within the New Homiletic relates to sermonic language. Every Venerable rehearsed this shift—from the literary to the oral and imagistic. The former of these qualities—the oral—was not new at all, but renewed within majority culture preaching and learned from Henry Mitchell and African American preaching. At the same time, Allen observes, the rhetoric of the New Homiletic has majored in "imagistic, storied language . . ."[27] Speaking for his colleagues, Lowry asserts, "We are moving from a print to a screen culture."[28] This shift, then, seems to be moving in two directions at the same time. The paradigm shift burst out of Enlightenment-era homiletics by recovering the assets of the oral culture while anticipating those of the postmodern culture. It was as if the New Homiletic found preaching long embedded in the Reformation Era's print culture and sought to retrieve the oral cast of Scripture and the Great Tradition.[29] At the same time, the New Homiletic decided to move ahead with the profound changes occurring in language and culture as the "broadcast culture" emerged and is now rapidly morphing into an even more imagistic "digital culture."[30]

"Unfolding": A Look Ahead

If this publication intends a review and assessment of the New Homiletic at midcareer, it is also fitting that we "anticipate the consequences" of this movement during its second half-life. Several foundational values are embedded within this Re(New)ed Homiletic that are enduring and, perhaps, may well become even more important to the church's ministry of proclamation in the future. These include:

1. *The Narrative "Stay Against Confusion."*[31] Whatever else resides within the New Homiletic's theological foundations, a commitment to the integrity of biblical narrative abides at the center. Absent this rootage in the biblical narratives, Christian faith and practice become cut-flower artifacts. To be sure, another eclipse of biblical narrative threatens from the ideological right and the left—with PowerPoint thematics dominating some evangelical preaching and deconstructionist approaches luring some progressive preaching. The narrative commitments of the New Homiletic are a bold, countercultural stay against confusion from both ideological extremes.

2. *An Enduring Commitment to the Scriptural Text.* In the face of calls that the content of the church's proclamation "is not a text (and therefore scripture) but the world of the gospel,"[32] the New Homiletic remains mostly insistent that gospel and scriptural texts may not remain programmatically divorced. A notion of "gospel," in fact, that is not grounded within the particularities of biblical narratives will become a kind of Rorschach inkblot for "creative" preachers. However, it is likely that many African American preachers will continue to beseech the listeners in a "prayer of humble access" as the sermon begins that a text has been chosen (or has chosen the preacher). Even David Buttrick—who is among those joining Edward Farley in the former's "new paradigm"—posits a text of Scripture either as the structural plotting of the sermon (in the mode of immediacy) or as the nearby originating wellspring for the sermon's interest and intention (in the mode of reflectivity). Only the mode of praxis, then, allows for the "gospel, but not text"

approach to the sermon. The New Homiletic, on the other hand, will continue to insist that the proclamation of proclaiming the gospel be married to a rabbinic love for and deep engagement with scripture.

3. *Other "Unfoldings."* These will become evident as this mature stage of the New Homiletic's lifespan continues to develop. In retrospect, however, we are just beginning to learn how radical its initial steps were. And we may yet learn to preach this renewed hearing.[33]

Notes

Introduction: O. Wesley Allen Jr.

1. Richard L. Eslinger, *A New Hearing: Living Options in Homiletical Method* (Nashville: Abingdon, 1987).

2. See O. A. Dieter, "Arbor Picta: The Medieval Tree of Preaching," *Quarterly Journal of Speech* 51 (1965): 123–55.

3. Harry Emerson Fosdick, "What Is The Matter with Preaching?" *Harper's Magazine* (July 1928), 133–41; the article is reprinted and the question revisited in Mike Graves, ed., *What's the Matter with Preaching Today* (Louisville: Westminster John Knox, 2004).

4. R. E. C. Browne, *The Ministry of the Word* (London: SCM, 1958).

5. H. Grady Davis, *Design for Preaching* (Philadelphia: Muhlenberg, 1958).

6. Ibid., 1.

7. Ibid., 9.

8. Ibid., 15.

9. See Ludwig Wittgenstein, *Tractatus Logico-Philosophicus*, trans. C. K. Ogden (London: Routledge, 1922; original German ed. published in 1919), and *Philosophical Investigations*, 3rd ed., trans. G. E. M. Anscombe (New York: Macmillan, 1958; original German ed. published in 1953); Martin Heidegger, *On the Way to Language*, trans. Peter D. Hertz (San Francisco: Harper & Row, 1971; original German ed. published in 1959).

10. See Rudolf Bultmann, *New Testament and Mythology and Other Basic Writings*, sel., ed., and trans. Schubert M. Ogden (Philadelphia: Fortress Press, 1984).

11. See James M. Robinson and John B. Cobb Jr., eds., *The New Hermeneutic*, New Frontiers in Theology, vol. II (New York: Harper & Row, 1964); Paul Achtemeier, *Introduction to the New Hermeneutic* (Philadelphia: Westminster, 1969).

12. Amos N. Wilder, *Early Christian Rhetoric: The Language of the Gospel* (London: SCM, 1964).

13. Marshall McLuhan, *The Gutenberg Galaxy: The Making of Typographic Man* (Toronto: University of Toronto Press, 1962); Walter J. Ong, *The Presence of the Word: Some Prolegomena for Cultural and Religious History* (New Haven: Yale University Press, 1967); and idem, *Orality and Literacy: The Technologizing of the Word* (New York: Routledge, 1982).

14. http://www.homiletics.org/members/pdfmembers/Randolph.pdf, accessed November 9, 2009 (member-only Web site).

15. Charles L. Rice, *Interpretation and Imagination: The Preacher and Contemporary Literature* (Philadelphia: Fortress Press, 1970).

16. Edmund A. Steimle, Morris J. Niedenthal, and Charles L. Rice, *Preaching the Story* (Philadelphia: Fortress Press, 1980)

17. Henry H. Mitchell, *Black Preaching* (Philadelphia: Lippincott, 1970).

18. Henry H. Mitchell, *The Recovery of Black Preaching* (San Francisco: Harper & Row, 1977); Mitchell combined and revised the materials from *Black Preaching* and *The Recovery of Black Preaching* in a volume entitled *Black Preaching: The Recovery of a Powerful Art* (Nashville: Abingdon, 1990).

19. Mitchell later drew together strands of this theme from earlier work and expanded it in *Celebration and Experience in Preaching* (Nashville: Abingdon, 1990).

20. Fred Craddock, *As One without Authority* (Nashville: Abingdon, 1971).

21. Fred Craddock, *Overhearing the Gospel: Preaching and Teaching the Faith to Persons Who Have Heard it All Before* (Nashville: Abingdon, 1978).

22. Eugene Lowry, *The Homiletical Plot: The Sermon a Narrative Art Form* (Atlanta: John Knox, 1980).

23. David Buttrick, *Homiletic: Moves and Structures* (Philadelphia: Fortress Press, 1987).

Chapter 1: Charles L. Rice

1. See Charles L. Rice, "The Expressive Style in Preaching," *Princeton Seminary Bulletin* 64, no. 1 (March 1971): 30–42, and an elaboration of that, "The Preacher as Storyteller," *Union Seminary Quarterly Review* 31, no. 3 (Spring 1976): 182–97.

2. Joseph Sittler, *The Anguish of Preaching* (Philadelphia: Fortress Press, 1966), 8.

3. Charles L. Rice, *The Embodied Word: Preaching as Art and Liturgy*, Fortress Resources for Preaching (Minneapolis: Fortress Press, 1991).

4. Yngve Brilioth, *A Brief History of Preaching* (Philadelphia: Fortress Press, 1965).

5. See the documentary *Ozawa*, a film by David Maysles, Albert Maysles, Ellen Hovde, Susan Froemke, and Deborah Dickson (Sony Classical, 1985).

6. W. H. Auden, "Epistle to a Godson," in *Epistle to a Godson, and Other Poems* (New York: Random House, 1972).

7. H. H. Farmer, *The Servant of the Word*, The Preacher's Paperback Library (Philadelphia: Fortress Press, 1964 [1942]).

8. Wade Clark Roof and William McKinney, *American Mainline Religion: Its Changing Shape and Future* (New Brunswick, N.J.: Rutgers University Press, 1987), 56. They also cite the Gallup poll there.

9. See Richard Eslinger, *A New Hearing: Living Options in Homiletic Method* (Nashville: Abingdon, 1987), 18, where he quotes Charles Rice's 1979 article, "Just Church Bells? One Man's View of Preaching Today."

10. L. Susan Bond, *Trouble with Jesus: Women, Christology, and Preaching* (St. Louis: Chalice, 1999), 26.

11. See Phillips Brooks, *Lectures on Preaching* (New York: Dutton, 1886), 5; these are Brooks's 1877 Beecher Lectures.

12. This point is developed in Mary Alice Mulligan and Ronald Allen, "Help Us Figure Out What God Wants," chap. 1 of *Make the Word Come Alive: Lessons from Laity* (St. Louis: Chalice, 2005), esp. 5–9.

Chapter 2: Fred B. Craddock

1. John A. Broadus, *On the Preparation and Delivery of Sermons*, new & rev. ed. by Jesse Burton Weatherspoon (New York: Harper & Brothers, 1944).

2. Domenico Grazzo, *Proclaiming God's Message* (South Bend: University of Notre Dame Press, 1965).

3. J. L. Austin, *How to Do Things with Words: The William James Lectures Delivered at Harvard University in 1955*, ed. J. O. Urmson (Oxford: Clarendon, 1962).

4. James Bryant Conant, *Two Modes of Thought: My Encounters with Science and Education* (New York: Trident, 1964).

5. Amos Wilder, "The Word as Address and the Word as Meaning," in *The New Hermeneutic*, ed. James M. Robinson and John B. Cobb (New York: Harper & Row, 1964), 198–218.

6. C. H. Dodd, *The Parables of the Kingdom* (New York: Scribner's, 1961), 5.

Chapter 3: Henry H. Mitchell

1. As slightly paraphrased from *The Recovery of Preaching*, Ministers Paperback Library (New York: Harper & Row, 1977), 8–9.

2. Frank A. Thomas, *They Never Like to Quit Praisin' God* (Cleveland: Pilgrim, 1997).

3. In gratitude for their ministry(ies), I dedicate this essay to Professor Henry Mitchell and to the memory of Professor Ella P. Mitchell (1917–2008). Their remarkable marriage is described in their *Together for Good: Lessons from Fifty-Five Years of Marriage* (Kansas City: Andrews McMeel, 1999).

4. As indicative of Mitchell's place in scholarship and preaching, he has been feted with two books of essays written in his honor: Martha J. Simmons, ed., *Preaching on the Brink: The Future of Homiletics* (Nashville: Abingdon, 1996); and Samuel K. Roberts, ed., *Born to Preach: Essays in Honor of the Ministry of Henry and Ella Mitchell* (Valley Forge: Judson, 2000).

5. Among Mitchell's most enduring works in this regard are *Black Preaching*, C. Eric Lincoln Series on Black Religion (Philadelphia: Lippincott, 1970); *The Recovery of Preaching* (see n. 1 above); *Black Church Beginnings: The Long Hidden Realities of the First Years* (Grand Rapids: Eerdmans, 2004); and *Celebration and Experience in Preaching*, rev. ed. (Nashville: Abingdon, 2008; cf. original ed., 1990).

6. For example, in *Black Preaching: The Recovery of Powerful Art* (Nashville: Abingdon, 1990), Mitchell presumes that much African American preaching should take place in "the mother tongue of the Spirit," that is, black English (76–87). Students at Christian Theological Seminary report that while that situation continues to be true in some African American congregations, other congregations today are more at home with language patterns that move in the direction of English that is a hybrid between African American and European American cultures or even majority-culture English. Mitchell himself notes, "The day will undoubtedly come when the barriers have fallen to the extent that there is virtually one tongue" (ibid., 87).

7. A theory arising from an empirical study of listeners finds that people tend to be moved in one of three ways—some by relationships, others by ideas, and still others by feeling. See Ronald J. Allen, *Hearing the Sermon: Relationship, Content, Feeling* (St. Louis: Chalice, 2004).

8. I regard the designation "New Homiletic" as unfortunate. How "new" will it seem in thirty years? In my lifetime (born 1949), for instance, the title "new" in the new quest of the historical Jesus of the 1960s and 1970s and the "New Hermeneutic" of the same time period now sounds quaint and dated. When naming movements that are contemporaneous with them, scholarship would be better served by names that emphasize not the time period of the movement but by its chief characteristics.

9. Throughout his ministry, Mitchell has sought to keep close to "the folk." For example, see his *Black Belief: Folk Beliefs of Blacks and America and West Africa* (New York: Harper & Row, 1975); and, with Nicholas C. Cooper-Lewter, *Soul Theology: The Heart of American Black Culture* (Nashville: Abingdon, 1991).

10. A research project awaits an eager doctoral student in assessing the relationship between the New Homiletic and this decline.

11. The Emergent Church is attempting to preach in modes of communication that are at home in popular cultures in North America. For an example, see Doug Pagitt, *Preaching Re-Imagined* (Grand Rapids: Zondervan, 2005). A theological question that all such efforts face is the degree to which a culture and its forms co-opt and compromise the church's deepest theological convictions.

Chapter 4: Eugene L. Lowry

1. Eugene L. Lowry, *The Homiletical Plot: The Sermon as Narrative Art Form* (Atlanta: John Knox, 1980).

2. Eugene L. Lowry, *Doing Time in the Pulpit: The Relationship between Narrative and Preaching* (Nashville: Abingdon, 1985).

3. H. Grady Davis, *Design for Preaching* (Philadelphia: Fortress Press, 1958), 164.

4. Walter Brueggemann, *Finally Comes the Poet: Daring Speech for Proclamation* (Minneapolis: Fortress Press, 1989), 68.

5. Walter J. Ong, *Orality and Literacy: The Technologizing of the Word*, New Accents (New York: Routledge, 1982), 132.

6. Thomas H. Troeger, *Imagining a Sermon*, Abingdon Preacher's Library (Nashville: Abingdon, 1990), 39–47.

7. Davis, *Design for Preaching*, 203–09.

8. Ibid., 163–69.

9. James Earl Massey, *Designing the Sermon: Order and Movement in Preaching* (Nashville: Abingdon, 1980), 20. See also idem, *The Responsible Pulpit* (Anderson, Ind.: Warner Press, 1974), 79–80.

10. David James Randolph, *The Renewal of Preaching* (Philadelphia: Fortress Press, 1969), 5–6, 16.

11. Eugene L. Lowry, *The Sermon: Dancing the Edge of Mystery* (Nashville: Abingdon, 1997), 29–38. See Henry H. Mitchell, *The Recovery of Preaching* (New York: Harper & Row, 1977), 11–29.

12. Lowry, *The Sermon*, 24–25.

13. Ibid., 36.

14. Ibid., 61.

15. Fred B. Craddock, *As One without Authority* (Nashville: Abingdon, 1979), 70.

16. Lowry, *The Sermon*, 26–28.

17. Ibid., 60.

18. Eunjoo M. Kim, *Preaching the Presence of God: A Homiletic from an Asian American Perspective* (Valley Forge: Judson, 1999), 121–25.

Chapter 5: David Buttrick

1. The new homiletic was named by David J. Randolph in *The Renewal of Preaching* (Philadelphia: Fortress Press, 1969), and seems to include Fred B. Craddock, *As One without Authority: Essays on Inductive Preaching* (Enid, Okla.: Phillips University Press, 1971) and *Overhearing the Gospel* (Nashville: Abingdon, 1978); Henry H. Mitchell, *Black Preaching* (Philadelphia: Lippincott, 1970) and *The Recovery of Preaching* (San Francisco: Harper & Row, 1977); Charles L. Rice, *Interpretation and Imagination: The Preacher and Contemporary Literature* (Philadelphia: Fortress Press, 1970) and, with Edmund A. Steimle and Morris J. Niedenthal, *Preaching the Story* (Philadelphia: Fortress Press, 1980); Eugene L. Lowry, *The Homiletical Plot: The Sermon as Narrative Art Form* (Atlanta: John Knox, 1980) and *Doing Time in the Pulpit: The Relationship Between Narrative and Preaching* (Nashville: Abingdon, 1985); David Buttrick, *Homiletic: Moves and Structures* (Philadelphia: Fortress Press, 1987); and, on some lists, Thomas G. Long, *The Senses of Preaching* (Atlanta: John Knox, 1988) and *The Witness of Preaching* (Louisville: Westminster John Knox, 1989); and Paul Scott Wilson, *Imagination of the Heart: New Understandings in Preaching* (Nashville: Abingdon, 1988).

2. See Roland Bainton, *Here I Stand: A Life of Martin Luther* (Nashville: Abingdon-Cokesbury, 1950), 185.

3. René Descartes's "I think, therefore I am" appears first as "*Je pense, donc je suis*," in his *Discourse on Method* (1637), and subsequently as "*cogito ergo sum*" in his *Principles of Philosophy* (1644).

4. The phrase "the mighty acts of God" deliberately echoes the title of an influential work by George Ernest Wright, *God Who Acts: Biblical Theology as Recital* (London: SCM, 1952). See also J. Kenneth Kuntz, *The Self-Revelation of God* (Philadelphia: Westminster, 1967).

5. Albert Schweitzer, *The Quest of the Historical Jesus: A Critical Study of Its Progress from Reimarus to Wrede*. 2d Eng. ed., trans. W. Montgomery (London: Adam & Charles Black, 1911).

6. Philip Rieff, *The Triumph of the Therapeutic* (New York: Harper & Row, 1966).

7. Brevard Childs, *Biblical Theology in Crisis* (Philadelphia: Westminster, 1970).

8. Brevard Childs, "Interpreting the Bible Amid Cultural Change," in *Theology Today* 54, no. 3 (July 1977): 200–11.

9. William Makepeace Thackeray, *Vanity Fair: A Novel Without a Hero* (New York: P. F. Collier & Son, 1917).

10. I think the author was Edoardo Sanguinetti, but I have been unable to relocate the story.

11. Walker Percy, *The Moviegoer* (New York: Popular Library, 1962), 68. Not surprisingly, the episode was inspired by Søren Kierkegaard.

12. Here's a beginner's list: Martin Buber, *The Martin Buber Reader*, ed. Asher Biemann (New York: Palgrave Macmillan, 2002); Emmanuel Lévinas, *The Levinas Reader*, ed. Sean Hand (Oxford: Blackwell, 1989); Alfred Schütz, *The Phenomeology of the Social World*, trans. George Walsh and Frederick Lehnert. (Evanston: Northwestern University Press, 1967); Edward Farley, *Good and Evil: Interpreting a Human Condition.* (Minneapolis: Fortress Press, 1990); and Paul R. Sponheim, *Faith and the Other: A Relational Theology* (Minneapolis: Fortress Press, 1993). See also my *Preaching the New and the Now* (Louisville: Westminster John Knox, 1998), 75–78.

13. Tony Kushner, *Angels in America: A Gay Fantasia on National Themes, Part Two: Perestroika* (New York: Theatre Communications Group, 1994), 158.

14. P. T. Forsythe, *Positive Preaching and the Modern Mind*, ed. D. Hadidian (Pittsburgh: Pickwick, 1985) See also my review article, "P. T. Forsythe—The Man, the Preacher's Theologian, Prophet for the Twentieth Century," *Princeton Seminary Bulletin* (November 1985): 231–34.

15. H. Marshall McLuhan, *Understanding Media: The Extensions of Man* (New York: New American Library, 1964).

16. Walter J. Ong, S.J., *The Presence of the Word* (New Haven: Yale University Press, 1967).

17. Robert Browning, *Pippa Passes: A Drama*, in *The Poetic and Dramatic Works of Robert Browning* (New York: Houghton, Mifflin, 1898), 337–38.

18. Tennessee Williams, *The Night of the Iguana* (New York: Dramatists Play Service, Inc., 1991, on behalf of the University of the South, Sewanee, Tenn.), 34.

19. Tony Kushner, *Angels in America, Part Two: Perestroika*, 50–51.

20. Jean-François Lyotard, *The Postmodern Condition: A Report on Knowledge* (Minneapolis: University of Minnesota Press, 1984), xxiv.

21. Jean-François Lyotard, *La Postmodernidad: Explicada a los niños* (Barcelona: Editorial Gedisa, 1996), 31.

22. Lyotard, *The Postmodern Condition*, 60.

23. See Pablo A. Jiménez, *An Untimely Word: Reflections on Preaching in a Postmodern Time* (Austin: The Episcopal Theological Seminary of the Southwest, 1998).

24. Justo L. González, "Metamodern Aliens in a Postmodern Jerusalem," in *Hispanic/Latino Theology*, ed. Fernando F. Segovia and Ada María Isasi-Díaz (Minneapolis: Fortress Press, 1996), 396.

25. D. K. McKim and P. S. Chung, "Revelation and Scripture," in *Global Dictionary of Theology*, ed. William Dyrness and Veli-Matti Kärkkäinen (Downers Grove, Ill.: InterVarsity, 2008), 758.

26. Buttrick, *Homiletic*, 24.

Afterword: Richard L. Eslinger

1. Richard L. Eslinger, *A New Hearing: Living Options in Homiletic Method* (Nashville: Abingdon, 1987).

2. Reflecting the significant contributions made in the field of homiletics and the vast influence provided across the church, a number of the five scholars surveyed in *A New Hearing* have been the subject of collections of essays by their colleagues. These include *Preaching as a Theological Task: World, Gospel, Scripture: In Honor of David Buttrick*, ed. Thomas G. Long and Edward Farley (Louisville: Westminster John Knox, 1996); *Preaching on the Brink: The Future of Homiletics: In Honor of Henry H. Mitchell*, ed. Martha J. Simmons (Nashville: Abingdon, 1996); *Listening to the Word: Studies in Honor of Fred B. Craddock*, ed. Gail R. O'Day and Thomas G. Long (Nashville: Abingdon, 1993); *What's the Shape of Narrative Preaching? Essays in Honor of Eugene L. Lowry*, ed. Mike Graves and David J. Schlafer (St. Louis: Chalice, 2008). The current collection may be considered a further festschrift in honor of all five of these scholars!

3. See above, 96.

4. See Hans W. Frei, *The Eclipse of Biblical Narrative: A Study in Eighteenth and Nineteenth Century Hermeneutics* (New Haven: Yale University Press, 1974).

5. See Frank Thomas, *They Like to Never Quit Praisin' God: The Role of Celebration in Preaching* (Cleveland: United Church Press, 1997).

6. Amos N. Wilder, *Early Christian Rhetoric: The Language of the Gospel* (Cambridge: Harvard University Press, 1964).

7. Adolf Jülicher, *Die Gleichnisreden Jesu* (Freiburg: J.C.B. Mohr, 1899).

8. David Buttrick, *Homiletic: Moves and Structures* (Philadelphia: Fortress Press, 1987), 194.

9. I am indebted to David Buttrick for this comment gleaned from a recent conversation.

10. See Charles L. Rice, *The Embodied Word: Preaching as Art and Liturgy*, Fortress Resources for Preaching (Minneapolis: Fortress Press, 1991).

11. See above, 99.

12. See Richard Lischer, *The Preacher King: Martin Luther King, Jr. and the Word That Moved America* (New York: Oxford University Press, 1995).

13. See above, 8.

14. See above, 8.

15. See above, 110.

16. See Stanley Hauerwas's hermeneutic investigations of the various rabbit communities of Richard Adams's novel *Watership Down* in his *A Community of Character: Toward a Constructive Social Ethic* (Notre Dame, Ind.: University of Notre Dame Press, 1981), 9–35.

17. See above, 120.

18. See above, 64.

19. See above, 110.

20. See above, 117.

21. See above, 9.

22. Eugene Lowry, *Doing Time in the Pulpit: The Relationship between Narrative and Preaching* (Nashville: Abingdon, 1985).

23. Ibid., 27.

24. See above, 95.

25. Lowry adds that the reason for this heightened emphasis on the episodic quality of the homiletical plot is that "other contexts of communication in our time and culture also lean toward the episodal." See above, 95.

26. See above, 66.

27. See above, 9.

28. See above, 83.

29. By "Great Tradition," I mean "the process of living and worshiping in a community shaped over time by the whole story of God and the world—nature and history, heaven and earth together." Don E. Saliers, *Worship Come to Its Senses* (Nashville: Abingdon, 1996), 70.

30. See M. Rex Miller, *The Milennium Matrix: Reclaiming the Past, Reframing the Future of the Church* (San Francisco: Jossey-Bass, 2004).

31. Ron Hansen, *A Stay against Confusion: Essays on Faith and Fiction* (New York: HarperCollins, 2001).

32. Edward Farley, "Toward a New Paradigm for Preaching," in *Preaching as a Theological Task: World, Gospel, Scripture*, ed. Thomas G. Long and Edward Farley (Louisville: Westminster John Knox, 1996), 170. For an insightful critique and response to Farley, see Ronald J. Allen, "Why Preach from Passages in the Bible?," in *Preaching as a Theological Task*, 176–85.

33. I am indebted to Dale Andrews for this phrase.